10
COMMITMENTS™
FOR DADS

10
COMMITMENTS™
FOR DADS

JOSH McDOWELL

HARVEST HOUSE PUBLISHERS
EUGENE, OREGON

Cover by Dugan Design Group, Bloomington, Minnesota

Cover photo © Stockbyte / Getty Images

10 COMMITMENTS is a series trademark of The Hawkins Children's LLC. Harvest House Publishers Inc. is the exclusive licensee of the trademark 10 COMMITMENTS.

10 COMMITMENTS™ FOR DADS
Copyright © 2014 by Josh McDowell Ministry. All rights reserved.
Published by Harvest House Publishers
Eugene, Oregon 97402
www.harvesthousepublishers.com

Library of Congress Cataloging-in-Publication Data
McDowell, Josh.
10 commitments for dads / Josh McDowell.
    pages cm
Includes bibliographical references.
ISBN 978-0-7369-5384-9 (pbk.)
ISBN 978-0-7369-5386-3 (eBook)
1. Fatherhood—Religious aspects—Christianity. I. Title. II. Title: Ten commitments for dads.
BV4529.17.M334 2014
248.8'42—dc23
                                                                    2013017168

          14 15 16 17 18 19 20 21 22 / VP-JH / 10 9 8 7 6 5 4 3 2 1

I wish to recognize the following individuals for their valuable contribution to this book:

Dave Bellis, my friend and colleague for over 35 years, for collaborating with me on the outline of this book, pulling material from my talks and other works to write the rough draft, and folding in all the edits and revisions to shape this work into its final form. I recognize Dave's insights on the topic of dads and I'm deeply grateful for his contribution.

David Thurston for critiquing the manuscript and providing helpful input on making the book clearer and more easily understood.

Becky Bellis for laboring at the computer to ready the manuscript.

Joshua Devries for coordinating the production elements and digital tags that have enhanced this book.

Terry Glaspey of Harvest House for his vision and guidance in shaping the direction and tone of this work.

Paul Gossard of Harvest House for the expert editing and insight he brought to the manuscript completion.

Contents

Foreword *by Sean McDowell*
11

Chapter One
What's a Dad to Do?
13

Chapter Two
Commitment #1: I Will Do My Best to
Always Speak the Truth in Love
21

Chapter Three
Commitment #2: I Will Do My Best to
Be Responsible *to* My Kids Rather Than *for* Them
First Part
35

Chapter Four
Commitment #2: I Will Do My Best to
Be Responsible *to* My Kids Rather Than *for* Them
Second Part
47

Chapter Five
Commitment #3: I Will Do My Best to
Be an Authentic Model
61

Chapter Six
Commitment #4: I Will Do My Best to
Explain Who God Is and What He Is Like
71

Chapter Seven
Commitment #5: I Will Do My Best to
Instill a Love of Self That Is Unselfish
91

Chapter Eight
Commitment #6: I Will Do My Best to
Impart God's Way of Forming Healthy Love Relationships
105

Chapter Nine
Commitment #7: I Will Do My Best to
Instruct on How to Know Right from Wrong
119

Chapter Ten
Commitment #8: I Will Do My Best to
Teach How to Honor God's Design for Sex
135

Chapter Eleven
Commitment #9: I Will Do My Best to
Present Why We Believe What We Believe
149

Chapter Twelve
Commitment #10: I Will Do My Best to
Foster a Heart of Gratitude
165

Afterword
"I Will Do My Best"
173

Relational Needs Assessment Inventory
175

Notes
183

Foreword

by Sean McDowell

Being a father is tough business. While I love being a dad, I often find myself wanting to scream and pull my hair out and say, "I didn't sign up for this!" And yet I wouldn't trade it for the world.

My wife and I aim to be the best parents we can be, but when I'm at a loss, I often find myself wondering, *WWJD?* I don't mean "What Would Jesus Do?" It would be nice to have a direct line to Jesus on parenting, but the reality is he had very little to say about how to be a good dad. In fact, what he did say is quite controversial (for example, Luke 14:26).

By *WWJD*, I mean "What Would Josh Do?" Now, as my dad admits right at the beginning of this book, since he was a traveling speaker, my mom was more present in our daily lives than he was. Yet my parents were—and still are—a great team. I don't mean to imply they were perfect. That's certainly not the case. Dad made many mistakes, as he says in chapter 1. And by all sociological measurements, his life should be a wreck because of his terrible upbringing. (More about that in a minute.)

Despite his shortcomings, though, my dad gave us kids the love, direction, and boundaries we needed. And I hope to instill the same in my own three kids.

That's why I appreciate this book. It's not a simple list of do's and don'ts for dads that guarantees kids will turn out right, as if parenting were like baking a cake or planning a vacation (of course, we all know vacations don't always turn out as planned either!). We all know it's not that simple. Rather, this book is filled with examples of successes and failures from my dad's experiences, seasoned by biblical truth and including some practical steps as well.

One of the things I appreciate most about my father is how vulnerable he has been regarding the struggles in his own life. He continues that honesty in this book. Even though I had heard the stories about his alcoholic father, his broken family, and the sexual abuse, I'm not sure I fully realized how difficult it was until we were sitting down for dinner at a recent family gathering. Mom was sharing funny stories about her childhood, and my sister asked Dad to share one from his life. After an awkward pause he said, "I don't have any good memories at all." For some reason when he said that, it hit me harder than ever before. My dad couldn't even think of *one* good family memory. My heart was broken.

And yet there we were, decades after his childhood, with a close, loving family. How did this happen?

If you're wondering about the answer to that question, then this book is perfect for you. If anything, it's testimony that God can redeem even the most broken and dysfunctional family. Whether you're a new dad trying to function on minimal sleep or you've been parenting for years, you will find both hope and direction in *10 Commitments for Dads*. Enjoy!

Sean McDowell

1

What's a Dad to Do?

It felt like hours. I couldn't stop pacing. Dottie had been in the delivery room longer than I'd expected.

Back then there were no Lamaze classes and husbands weren't allowed to be a part of the birthing process with their wives in the hospital delivery room. Expectant dads were relegated to a waiting room to pace the floor. So that's what I was doing.

Finally they wheeled Dottie out of the delivery room holding an eight-pound, two-ounce baby girl. Once we got into the hospital room Dottie handed her to me. As I held Kelly my knees went weak. It dawned on me that now I was actually a father, but I didn't have a clue about fathering.

I wasn't really trained to be a father, and most of us aren't. It's natural to be running scared. Then when you look around and see the culture our kids face, you get petrified. Most of the values today's culture embraces are almost the opposite of what you want your kids to embrace. Kids are getting into drugs, alcohol, and sex at an earlier and earlier age. You read about the bullying, violence, and suicide that is happening among kids and it's cause for alarm. What's a dad to do?

How Did You Do It, Josh?

Many people know my childhood story. I was the son of the town drunk. He was abusive to my mother, kept drunk most of the time, and more or less ignored me. I never remember hearing my dad ever say he loved me. I guess I feared that my dysfunctional child-hood would somehow carry over into my own family, so I was run-ning scared.

I've had people come up to me and ask, "How'd you do it, Josh?" They see my four adult children—Kelly, Sean, Katie, and Heather—and wonder what we did to raise up such faithful Christian adults, now married and raising great families of their own. It appears that we did something right. I'd like to think we did all the right things, but we didn't. Frankly, I blew it a lot, but I kept at it. This book is a distilling of the commitments I made to God, myself, and my family in order to raise my kids to honor their parents and God. But before we walk through those commitments, let's tee them up—put them in the proper context.

1. A Dad Isn't Really Complete Without the Mom

My kids are where they are today relationally, spiritually, emo-tionally, and so on thanks largely to my wife, Dottie. I didn't default on my responsibility as a dad. I took it very seriously. The truth is, though, Dottie was the constant presence in their lives lovingly instructing them, guiding them, and being there for them. I have been a traveling speaker all my adult life, so I was away a lot. Dot-tie made the big difference in how she supported me in my father-ing role. She became the complementary eyes and ears and heart I needed. She could see things I couldn't. I needed her perspective. She could hear the tone of a voice—a tone I struggled to fully under-stand. I needed her insights. She could feel things with the heart that I couldn't quite sense. I needed her sensitivity. Reality was, my chil-dren's mother completed their dad.

I suspect that many moms are reading this book right now. Most books are read by women. First, I encourage you to urge your hus-band to read it. Second, be there for him as he attempts to embrace the 10 Commitments for Dads. He needs your support, encour-agement, respect, acceptance, comfort, approval, and appreciation throughout the process. You have a perspective on, insight into, and sensitivity to life and relationships he needs. That is the way God put us together. He has given each of us insights and abilities that the other needs, just like he has with his body, the church. "We are all parts of his one body," the apostle Paul said, "and each of us has different work to do. And since we are all one body in Christ, we belong to each other, and each of us needs all the others" (Romans 12:5 NLT).

Dad, look to your wife. You need her perhaps more than you realize in order to be an effective father. If your wife isn't reading this book, ask her to read it with you and help you be the father you want to be and the one God intends. Mom, you're a vital part of this process with your husband. Help him. He needs you in a big way.

If you're a single dad, don't be discouraged. Sure, it's tougher without your kids' mom being there with you. If you have an ex, do your best to live at peace with her, and make the best out of a less-than-ideal situation for the sake of the kids as much as possible. Latch onto another Christian couple within your church. As I said above, we as the body of Christ "belong to each other, and each of us needs all the others" (Romans 12:5 NLT). Ask them for help. Another couple can even read this book with you and give you added insights and support. Successfully raising children isn't to be done in isolation. God intended us to be there for one another to fulfill our responsibilities to each other and to our kids.

2. Make the Most of Your Time

My situation was probably different than yours. As I said, I have been a traveling speaker practically all my life. That means I was gone from home a lot. The downside of that is that I wasn't with my kids like I wanted to be. The upside was that it caused me to make the most of my time.

You may not realize it, but before you know it your kids will be out of your home and on their own. Time is flying by at lightning speed. The recurring theme among dads who are lamenting their disconnected relationship with their college-age kids now is, "I didn't take enough time with them when they were young."

The psalmist had it right: "Teach us to make the most of our time, so that we may grow in wisdom" (Psalm 90:12 NLT). I learned that when I was home I needed to pack in practically every waking moment with my kids. I wanted to make my time count. And when I did go on the road I would write my kids and call them. I wanted to be sure I was a presence in their lives even when I was away.

Make every day count. Be there for your kids. Be intentional about it. Put them in your schedule like a business appointment if you have to—just don't let time get away without being there for them.

3. Don't Underestimate Your Influential Role as a Dad

Recently a dad came up to me and said, "Josh, I simply can't compete. My kids are inundated by the media—iPhone, iPad, iTunes, texting, tweeting, e-mail, the Internet, movies, school, everything. They're learning everything from everyone but me. I don't stand a chance!"

A lot of dads feel that way, but they're dead wrong. With all of today's media and all the distractions your kids face, you are still the most important and most influential figure in your child's life.

A national online study shows that 45 percent of young people consider their parents to be their role models.[1] I suspect you thought today's musical sensations or young movie stars or sports celebrities were your kids' role models. But they're not. Other studies show that 32 percent of today's kids look to their friends and just 15 percent looked to celebrities for guidance and inspiration.[2] In fact, the studies show that even until your child reaches 25 years of age, the greatest influence on his or her behavior will be the loving, close relationship with you, the father.[3] Researchers at the University of Florida recently stated that "the good news is that most teens ARE listening to what parents are saying despite what they [the parents] think."[4]

Let's say your kids are listening, even though it seems at times they're not. Do you know what you want to say? Do you know what it is that you want for your kids—what you want to specifically instill in them?

4. Know What You Truly Want for Your Kids

You have probably heard it said, "A man who aims at nothing will always hit it." Or, "A man who doesn't know where he's going will always get there." That's true with parenting too. If we as dads don't know what it is we want to impart to our kids we are not likely to impart much at all.

We need to know where we are leading our kids or we can't very well get them there. Do you know what you want for your kids? Think about that for a second. When it comes right down to it, what do you want for that child you so dearly love?

You could probably come up with a lot of answers. But let's pose that same question to God. What does the Creator God who loves you so very much want for you? Some might think all he really wants is for you to follow his commandments—to serve and obey. Is that all you want from your kids—to do what you say? Children are commanded in Scripture to obey their parents, and God certainly wants you to obey him. But there is something more basic than that. God does want obedience, but for a very good reason.

Jesus had taught his followers all the laws of Moses. He wanted them to be devoted to him and the commands of Scripture. Yet he shared the bottom line of *why* he really wanted their devotion—and it applies to each of us too. He said, "I have told you this so my joy may be in you and that your joy may be complete" (John 15:11 NIV). That is what God wants for his children—to be filled with joy. That's what we want for our children too. We want to see them happy. We want them to enjoy life, be protected from harm, and become individuals with a sense of meaning, purpose, and fulfillment. And most of us probably believe that doing what is right will produce a life of joy. And we have good reason to believe that.

King David and his own son King Solomon wrote,

> Joyful are people of integrity, who follow the instructions of the LORD. Joyful are those who obey his laws and search for him with all their hearts (Psalm 119:1-2 NLT).

> Make me walk along the path of your commands, for that is where my happiness is found (Psalm 119:35 NLT).

> This is my happy way of life: obeying your commandments (Psalm 119:56 NLT).

> My child, listen to what I say, and treasure my commands. Tune your ears to wisdom, and concentrate on understanding...Then you will understand what is right, just and fair, and you will find the right way to go. For wisdom will enter your heart, and knowledge will fill you with joy. Wise choices will watch over you. Understanding will keep you safe (Proverbs 2:1-2,9-11 NLT).

Don't we as dads want our kids to realize that lasting joy in life is in understanding that God has given them a "right way to go" and the wisdom to make the right moral choices in life? We want them to mature into young men and women who can stand strong in the face of a hostile culture. Before they leave home we want to instill into them the kind of values and perspective about God and life that will give them a fighting chance to accomplish just that.

Again, that is what this book is all about. We want to journey together with you through 10 Commitments that can help you lead your kids to a life full of joy by helping them accomplish at least seven things in life before leaving home:

1. form a right relationship with God
2. develop healthy relationships with others
3. have a healthy self-image

4. resist sexual pressure

5. be a person of integrity

6. develop deepened convictions

7. know how to handle success and cope with failure

If your kids learn to accomplish those seven things their joy will be complete—and so will yours.

5. Your Commitments: More than Mere Interest, Yet Less than Solid Guarantees

Let me say this up front—there are no perfect dads in this world. You will not be able to keep the 10 Commitments listed in this book perfectly. You can even have perfect intentions to keep these commitments, yet you may not always live up to them. Any commitments you make to God, yourself, or your children should come from a deep longing and desire to fulfill them. But being human means you are imperfect.

Your commitments then are your heartfelt attempts to endeavor to always fulfill them and to earnestly strive to keep them. That means the commitments you make are not mere intentions or haphazard want-to's—they are more than that. Yet they are less than solid guarantees. With that in mind I am challenging you to make and *do your best* to fulfill these 10 Commitments for Dads.

As a Christian father you want your kids to be prepared for the hostile culture they will face. You are probably seeking to raise them up to live God-honoring lives filled with joy and happiness. You undoubtedly want to lead them to accomplish the seven things listed above. If so, you are ready for the challenge—a commitment to do your best to

1. always speak the truth in love

2. be responsible *to* your kids rather than *for* them

3. be an authentic (not perfect) model

4. explain who God is and what he is like

5. instill a love of self that is unselfish

6. impart God's way of forming healthy love relationships

7. instruct on how to know right from wrong

8. teach how to honor God's design for sex

9. present why we believe what we believe

10. foster a heart of gratitude

In the pages that follow we will take a journey together to explore how you can fulfill these 10 Commitments. Now that doesn't mean your children will turn out perfectly. No matter how perfect a dad you might be or how diligent you are to raise them up to love God, themselves, and others, they are the ones who make the final decision on the path they take. You can't make their choices for them. You can simply provide them the right foundation, a healthy model, and the training to choose the right path.

Passing your faith and values on to your kids isn't done in a weekend camping trip or six-week home Bible study. It happens by imparting these truths in the day-to-day, week-by-week, month-by-month interactions with your kids. It is about imparting certain truths about God and life and love and relationships very intentionally.

Moses told the children of Israel that they must love the Lord with all their hearts, soul, and strength and obey God's commandments. And then he said,

> Repeat them again and again to your children. Talk about them when you are at home, and when you are on the road, when you are going to bed and when you are getting up (Deuteronomy 6:7-8 NLT).

Do you get the idea that this was a continual process? It was then—and it still is a continual process for us today.

2

I Will Do My Best to
Always Speak the Truth in Love

Josh, what do I do about my kids?" the dad said as he clutched my arm. I had just finished speaking on parenting and this man sounded desperate. He said he had three children—17, 13, and 10—and, "They're the worst kids in my church and I'm the pastor."

"I've done everything I know to do," he went on. "I've taught them God's truth constantly. I've made them memorize Scripture. They know what is expected of them—I lay down the rules, but they are rebelling and they're ticked off at me most of the time. What do I do?"

This father was trying in every way to get his kids to do the right things. He didn't say it, but I'm sure he wanted them to be happy and knew their misbehavior would eventually cause them pain. We all want our kids to do right and avoid pain.

I touched him on his shoulder and looked directly into his eyes. "Brother, my advice to you is to back off the rules."

"What?" he responded in disbelief. "That's what's wrong—they're not obeying any rules now and they don't even think they need to!"

"I know what you're saying," I told him, "but I repeat, lay off emphasizing the rules."[1]

The Bible has a message for dads who are trying to teach their kids right but are ticking them off. "Fathers, do not provoke your children to anger by the way you treat them" (Ephesians 6:4 NLT). How we as dads treat our kids can "provoke" them to anger. That is what my pastor friend was doing—holding his kids to the rules but provoking them to anger in the process.

Now just what does the Bible mean when it says "provoke"? Ephesians 6 uses the Greek word *parorgizo*, which literally means to "arouse to wrath." The passage is telling dads not to tick their kids off by the way they deal with them. What we do and say and how we do it and say it can do this.

The New International Version says, "Fathers, do not *exasperate* your children…" J.B. Phillips translates this verse, "Fathers, don't *over-correct* your children or make it difficult for them to obey the commandment." And *The Living Bible* says: "Don't keep on *scolding and nagging* your children, making them angry and resentful." In another passage the Bible says: "Fathers, do not aggravate your children, or they will become discouraged" (Colossians 3:21 NLT). Scripture is making a clear point that we as dads are to treat our kids in such a way as to avoid angering them. Sure, the Bible commands children to obey their parents, but we dads have a pretty tough assignment of acting in a way to keep from ticking them off. With that said, how do we treat our kids to get a positive response versus a negative reaction?

Four Styles of Relating to Your Kids

As a Christian dad you want what's best for your kids. You probably sense that rules and instructions are part of the parenting process, but your kids may see some of them as restricting their fun. If that's the case, then dad is viewed as a "killjoy." Have you heard your kids say things like "You never let me do anything" or "I can never have fun anymore" or "You just don't understand"? The reality is that most of our kids don't understand why we restrict them. So enforcing the rules often creates tension, arguments, and conflict within the family. And it seems that the more rules that are laid down, the more conflict it creates with our kids.

We dads may not realize it but each of us has adopted a parenting style, and that style has to do with how we view parental authority and relationships. Your style was most likely influenced by how your parents enforced or didn't enforce the rules when you were growing up and the kind of relationship they had with you. So how we view rules and relationships largely determines how we treat our kids.

The High-Control Dad

"Have you finished your homework yet?" "Did you take out the trash like I told you?" "You were supposed to be in by 10 p.m. Were you?" These are the types of questions a high-control dad would ask. But it's really not the line of questioning that makes up this style of parenting, it's the person's attitude toward the use of authority. The high-control parents, or *autocratic* parents as they are sometimes called, require strict obedience to the rules. You may know of a dad who controls his kids by intimidation or by force. It's a "You'll do it my way, or else!" approach.

In extreme cases autocratic dads wield absolute power over children, which often results in emotional and physical abuses. Yet many autocratic fathers who are less extreme in enforcing the rules can give children what appear to be "good homes." They feed and clothe their kids well, let them play with other children, and in short, seem to provide everything needed for a "normal life."

While they would never beat their children or lock them away in seclusion for disobedience, autocratic dads still reign as the enforcers. They are very big on rules, but low on relationships. Think of a teeter-totter with one end high in the air with a big emphasis on rules and the other end on the ground, low on relationships.

The High-Control Dad:
High on Rules, Low on Relationships

Living in an autocracy causes kids to react in one of two ways: *flight* or *fright*. But in each case the response is typically anger. When children choose *flight*, they may not literally run away from home, but they withdraw emotionally and relationally. They learn to go it alone and "be obedient"—at least on the surface. Inside, however, they are probably seething. You may have heard the story of the child whose father told him to sit down. The boy didn't want to sit down and made his feeling known to his dad. At that point the father yelled, "Sit down or I'll make you sit down!"

The boy quickly obeyed, but as he sat down he muttered under his breath, "I may be sitting down on the outside, but on the inside I'm standing up!" Forced obedience at the hand of a high-control dad rarely produces a child who is motivated to do what is right, even when they quietly comply with the rules. A dominated child is a frustrated and angry child on the inside.

However, when kids choose to *fight*, their anger is out in the open. That was the case with my pastor friend, whose kids were in open rebellion. His kids saw the rules clearly and how they were being enforced and didn't like it at all. Think about it. How do you respond to rules you see as restricting your freedom and fun? We all naturally resist rules for rules' sake. That's the way we were created. Rules were never meant to be used outside of a loving relationship.

The Anything-Goes Dad

Some dads who have been ruled by autocratic parents end up replicating the same approach with their kids. Some on the other hand overcompensate and practically toss out all the rules. They end up parenting in an anything-goes style, often referred to as *permissive* parenting.

A permissive dad is on a teeter-totter that's the opposite from the high-control dad's teeter-totter. The rules side of the fulcrum is down and the relational side is up. However, the relational approach of an anything-goes dad results in superficial and unhealthy relationships. The child generally ends up feeling, *My dad really doesn't care.*

The Anything-Goes Dad:
High on Relationships (Unhealthy Ones), but Low on the Rules

You have probably heard or seen permissive dads in action. Actually, the child is the one in action while the dad sort of stands and watches his kid destroy toys, flower beds, furniture, and the tranquility and peace of the household in general.

Permissively parented kids often hold their parents hostage. There was one dad who was frantically trying to get his four-year-old son to get in the car, but the boy was having too much fun on the swing. "Come on, Johnny, we've got to go now. Please get in the car," the father pleaded. His child didn't respond. After a minute or two the dad repeated his plea. Still no response. More minutes ticked by. Finally the dad said sternly, "Listen to me, Jonathan David—I'm not going to tell you but about ten more times to get into this car!"

Anything-goes-parented children get their way a lot, but they are no happier than the children in the autocratic homes because the balance of rules and relationships is not there. Frankly, the lack of rules causes the child to think, *If my dad really cared about me, he'd be more interested in what I do…he would say no sometimes…I guess he doesn't really love me.*

The Inattentive Dad

Another style of parenting is one of inattentiveness, sometimes called the *indifferent* style. This is the absentee dad who is just too busy with his life or his career and is not really involved in his child's world. A dad may be indifferent out of fear of failure, but for whatever reason his kids feel left out of his life. When children are parented indifferently, they can become hurt and angry. That was me—the kid whose dad was always too drunk to give any attention to his young son.

It was a Saturday morning. I was 11 years old. I dressed before dawn and hurriedly got my morning chores done before the workmen arrived.

A team of men had been working for days to jack up a small house on my parents' farm, preparing it to be moved to a new location. My grown brother, Wilmont, was having it moved over the objections of my father. Wilmont had been engaged in a bitter feud with my dad, which had escalated into an all-out war for half of the family farm. Having successfully sued my father, Wilmont had arrived that morning with a sheriff, a deputy, and a court order authorizing him to move the house.

I, however, was trying hard to stay out of the family conflict. I hated to see my dad and brother fight, but that was between them. Today I just wanted to savor the excitement of watching an entire house being towed down the road, a spectacle more entertaining to an 11-year-old mind than a traveling circus.

Then, just as the tractors were being attached to the house, my father, drunk as usual, began yelling at Wilmont. The sheriff moved quickly toward the staggering man to prevent an ugly scene.

But it was too late for that. My brother, expecting something like this, had arranged for numerous families from our small farming community to be on hand to provide moral support for him. Many of them began chanting obscenities at my father as the sheriff restrained the old man.

I watched in horror, my excitement turning to embarrassment. Frightened by the escalating conflict and humiliated to see our family's feud played out in full view of my friends and neighbors, I ran from the shameful scene and into our nearby barn. Slamming the door behind me, I scrambled into the corn bin and buried myself up to my neck in corn.

Dark, quiet, and alone, my shame slowly turned to anger. I was angry that my father's drinking had brought such division to my home. I was angry that he was rarely sober. And I was angry that he had caused such pain in my mother's life. But more than anything, I felt alone.

I lay there in the corn for what must have been hours. No one came looking for me. My dad didn't even notice I was gone. I felt forgotten. I felt like a nobody.

The Inattentive Dad:
Low on Relationships and Low on the Rules

Rules   Relationships

Inattentiveness or noncommunication says to a kid, "You're not worth much. You're not important. You're a nonentity." And again the hurt most likely represents itself inwardly as resentment or outwardly as rage.

The Loving Dad

This last parenting style is simply the *loving approach*. This kind of dad sees his child's best interest as his highest priority. It isn't so much a balancing act of trying to get the right number of rules and relationships measured out. Rather, it is a dad placing rules within the context of his loving relationship with his children. This way kids soon learn that rules come out of a heart of love to protect them from harm and provide for their well-being.

The pastor with the rebellious and angry kids had a problem. But it wasn't so much a kid problem—it was a dad problem. I would have liked to ask this dad a question: "Do your kids know why you are laying down all the rules?" I doubt if his kids knew. And I'm not sure he knew why he was so high on rule-setting either.

But when we place rules within the context of relationships, this offers a very good reason: rules are meant to provide and protect.

After the apostle Paul instructs dads not to provoke their kids to anger, he goes on to say, "Rather bring them up with the discipline and instruction that comes from the Lord" (Ephesians 6:4 NLT). The Lord's discipline always has the person's best interest at heart. The writer of Hebrews said, "The Lord disciplines those he loves…God's discipline is always good for us" (Hebrews 12:6,10 NLT).

If our kids are getting upset and angry and are resisting our rules—rules that are for their own good—then laying off emphasizing those rules may not make a lot of sense on the surface. It would seem that hammering home the rules even harder would be the more effective solution. But generally that will do nothing but increase their anger and resentment. What our kids need to see is that our rules are out of a heart of love and are actually good for them, just as the instructions and commands that come from God. We as dads need to learn how to place God's truth and family rules squarely within the context of our loving relationships.

The Loving Dad:
Rules Within the Context of a Loving Relationship

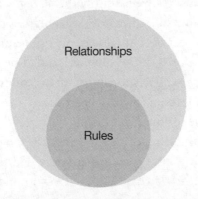

How to Speak the Truth

Earlier in the book of Ephesians, the apostle Paul used the phrase "speak the truth in love" (4:15 NLT). What he meant was that truth and rules were to always come from a heart of a loving relationship. The very reason you want your kids to follow certain rules is because that is what's best for them. Because you love them you want them to obey the rules. However, most kids will tend to see the rules and miss the relational context. There's a good reason for that.

Regardless of our parenting style, most of us men are wired to see life in a more logical and rational manner than women do. This isn't a hard-and-fast rule, but generally dads aren't "warm and fuzzy"— typically they're not intuitively relational. This isn't to say men find it hard to develop friendships or don't enjoy relational connection— most do. Yet it doesn't seem to come natural to most of us to see truth and rules within the solid context of relationship. Many of us would say that rules are rules and they need to be obeyed regardless of the relationship, right?

The truth is, God designed us to follow the rules *because* of the relationship. There are do's and don'ts in life, but they are there to provide for our well-being and protect us from harm. That's what a person within a loving relationship wants to do—protect those they love and provide for their best.

Why do you tell your kids, "Don't touch the stove," "Look both ways before crossing the street," or "Drive the speed limit"? Those do's and don'ts come out of love for your children. You put them in place because you don't want your kids to get hurt. Take those instructions out of a relational context, and they may seem like restrictions designed to take the fun out of life.

That is why we as dads must consistently and intentionally tie every rule we give our kids to our unfailing love for them. That is what God has done for us—yet we so often miss it. He isn't a high-control rule-enforcer who's looking over our shoulder to catch us doing something wrong. He isn't a permissive or inattentive God either. He is a loving God, who wants the very best for us. King David said, "Declare me innocent, O LORD, for I have acted with integrity…For I am always aware of your unfailing love and I have lived according to your truth" (Psalm 26:1,3 NLT). David saw God's truth within the context of his unfailing love. Our God is a loving God, who gave you and me guidelines in which relationships flourish and grow. The rules are there to create the fertile ground for healthy relationships to develop. That is what I worked hard to communicate to my kids.

"Dad, I'm having a great time here," Kelly said, her voice oozing with excitement. I pressed my finger to my ear and held the phone close to my listening ear. "It's hard to hear you, honey," I said. "Speak up a little."

The voices in the background were those of Kelly's eighth-grade classmates celebrating their graduation at her friend's house. "Sarah wants me to spend the night," Kelly yelled above the party noise. "Is that okay?" I asked a few questions and discovered that a number of boys were staying at the party past ten o'clock. And there were no guarantees that the boys weren't "smuggling" in some beer.

"I think it's best that you come home right after the party," I told my daughter. "But Dad," Kelly protested, "Sarah's parents are here and they're really watching out for us and stuff." "I know they're good people," I responded, "but I'm not comfortable with some of the boys who are there." Some of the names of the boys Kelly had relayed to me were known in the community as beer-drinking party animals. And I wasn't about to let her spend the night with that kind of crowd lingering in the shadows.

Kelly called back three times in the next half hour. At one point she began to cry, and then I learned what was really going on. A number of Kelly's friends also wanted to sleep over, but they too had to get their parents' permission. The strategy was to get Kelly McDowell's dad to say yes and then they would say to their parents, "Josh McDowell is letting Kelly sleep over." But I stood firm.

"Kelly, you need to be home by ten," I stated with no hesitation in my voice. "Okay, okay," she said as her voice cracked. I hung up with my daughter's sniffles clearly audible. I hated disappointing her, even though I knew what I was requiring of her was in her best interest.

The rules and restrictions I've given my kids were consciously intended to benefit them. It wasn't a control thing with me. It's not with God either. Every command, instruction, and rule that he gives us is for a relational purpose—it is for our good. After Jesus gave a set of instructions to his followers he said, "You know these things—now do them! That is the path of blessing" (John 13:17 NLT).

As I've said, God's rules are given to provide for our best interest and protect us from harm. Moses told the children of Israel to "always obey the LORD's commands and decrees that I am giving you today for your own good" (Deuteronomy 10:13 NLT). Each command God gives comes out of this loving motivation to provide for and protect us. And the commands we give to our kids should come out of the same motivation, and we need to make sure they know that. When we do we are raising "them up with the discipline and instruction that comes from the Lord" (Ephesians 6:4 NLT).

When I told Kelly to come home at ten and not sleep over at the graduation party, I wasn't saying that for my benefit. I wasn't getting a charge out of laying down the law. It was for her benefit. I was looking out for the best interest of my daughter. I wanted to protect her from harmful influences and provide her a healthier environment in which to develop emotionally, relationally and spiritually. And the great thing about it is, she realized that.

When she came home that night Dottie and I had already gone to bed. But she came into our room and woke us up to thank us for telling her she couldn't stay overnight. "Dad," she said, "I didn't really want to stay in the first place. The other girls were really pressuring me to get you to say yes because they thought it would get their parents to say yes. So you actually gave me the reason I needed to leave. Thanks for helping me out."

What a Loving Relationship Really Means

The next day I reinforced with Kelly that what I really wanted to do was protect her from damaging influences and provide for her best. I told her I'd do anything—sacrifice my time and energy, even my own life for her—because I loved her so much. That is the nature of true love—it looks out for the best interest of others. The Bible says, "Love is patient and kind. Love is not jealous or boastful or proud or rude. It does not demand its own way" (1 Corinthians 13:4-5 NLT). In other words, real love is unselfish.

Jesus said, "Do to others whatever you would like them to do to you" (Matthew 7:12 NLT); "Love your neighbor as yourself" (Matthew 22:39); and "Just as I have loved you, you should love each other" (John 13:34). The apostle Paul described such unselfish love this way: "Value others above yourselves, not looking to your own interests but each of you to the interests of others" (Philippians 2:4 NIV). When Paul applied this instruction to husbands he said for them "to love their wives as they love their own bodies…No one hates his own body but feeds and cares for it" (Ephesians 5:28-29).

This kind of unselfish love feeds, nourishes, and provides for others and also cherishes and protects them. From these and other verses we can define what a loving relationship really means. Truly loving someone means *making the security, happiness, and welfare of the person as important as your own.*

Do your kids know you love them like that? Don't assume they do without telling them often. I sensed that my friend's three rebellious children didn't really know their dad loved them that way. That is why I told him to back off the rules. I went on to tell him to work on the relationship. He needed to demonstrate again and again that their individual security, happiness, and welfare were as important to him as his own. That is what speaking the truth in love is all about.

Sit down with your kids and tell them you want nothing more than to see them happy. Explain that everything you do and say is an attempt—as imperfect as your attempts are at times—to protect them from harm and provide for their best. Share from the heart. Let your kids feel your caring heart so they connect with you on a relational level.

A number of years ago Dartmouth Medical School commissioned a scientific study of young people. The project, which was called "Hardwired to Connect," analyzed the results of more than 260 studies of youth. The report stated that 100 percent of all the studies they analyzed showed one thing: from the moment a baby is born his or her brain is physically, biologically, and chemically hardwired to connect with others in relationships. Dr. Allan Schore, highly respected expert at the UCLA School of Medicine, supports the conclusion: "We are born to form attachments. Our brains are physically wired to develop in tandem with another through emotional communication before words are spoken." [2]

Truth, by God's design, was meant to be learned and experienced within the context of a loving relationship. Rules given within the loving atmosphere of relationships will most likely bring a positive response. But if you come down hard with rules and restrictions without your kids feeling emotionally secure in your love, you should expect anger, resentment, and frustration (the lot of the high-control dad). Give your kids whatever they want whenever they want it and you'll exasperate them (the lot of the anything-goes dad). Get caught up in the busyness of life and be an absentee dad and your kids will feel like nobodies and become resentful (the lot of the inattentive dad).

However, if you place your instructions and rules within the context of a loving relationship so your kids know that all you do and say is meant for their protection and provision, you'll get a positive response (the lot of the loving dad). This is what Commitment #1 is all about—doing your best to always speak the truth in the context of a loving relationship.

3

COMMITMENT #2

I Will Do My Best to Be Responsible *to* My Kids Rather Than *for* Them

First Part

Y ou two boys straighten up," Mrs. Carlson bellowed, "or you're going to the principal's office right now!" The two rowdy fifth-graders had just been raked over the coals for not doing their homework. Now they were getting bawled out for disrupting the class.

My son, Sean, was a few desks over from the two troublemakers. They were actually his soccer teammates. But the two didn't much care for him. They weren't outright hostile toward him, but he definitely didn't feel welcome around them.

Sean wanted to impress the "tough guys" and perhaps be seen as a "tough guy" too. He decided to let those two boys know he was on their side. He thought a show of defiance toward the teacher would do the trick. So when Mrs. Carlson turned around to write something on the board, Sean gave her a one-finger salute. Well, that got him noticed.

Right after class, all the kids, including his two teammates, gathered around him and treated him like a celebrity. Problem was, word got back to Dottie and me of what he had done in class, and consequently he lost his celebrity status. Let me explain.

I admit the incident was a little embarrassing for me. I could have come down hard on Sean for reflecting badly on me. I could have come off with an "I have a reputation to protect and an image to uphold" attitude. If I had, I would have fallen into the self-centered trap of thinking my kid's behavior was really about me. And that would lead me to feel responsible *for* Sean's actions. But actually I wasn't responsible for what he did or didn't do. None of us dads are responsible for what our kids do.

Now that may sound foreign to some of you. Many fathers feel they *are* responsible for their kids' actions. It's almost as if they feel that what their kids do, good or bad, reflects on their own parenting performance. And in one way it does. Our kids do bear our last name, and people do tend to cast blame or give credit for how our kids behave. However, each person makes individual choices and he or she alone is responsible for his or her actions.

"Pay careful attention to your own work," the apostle Paul said, "for then you will get the satisfaction on a job well done, and you won't need to compare yourself to anyone else. For we are each responsible for our own conduct" (Galatians 6:4-5). People make choices, and kids are people too. You and I are not responsible for other people's choices.

Even the almighty and powerful God is not responsible for human behavior. He allows each of us to choose for ourselves whether we do right or wrong. We also must choose whether to have a loving relationship with him or not. He did this from the very beginning with Adam and Eve. This first relationship was based on an authentic love that was to be expressed freely and voluntarily. The first couple was free to choose, and with that choice God took a risk.

The risk was that Adam and Eve could choose to reject God's rule, which was given within the context of a loving relationship. Authentic love could not be forced. God knew they had to choose to love him back. He also knew the devastating consequences if they rejected him. That is why the very hint of his created humans trying to satisfy their needs outside of him produced jealousy. In one of the Scripture passages where his first commandment is recorded, it reads, "Do not worship any other god, for the LORD, whose name is Jealous, is a jealous God" (Exodus 34:14 NIV). The 1996 New Living Translation renders "a jealous God" as "a God who is passionate about his relationship with you."[1]

God in his holy jealousy looks out for our good. He simply doesn't want to see us suffer the negative consequences of our wrong choices. That is why he gave us instructions, commands, and certain rules to follow. As we stated in the last chapter, these guidelines serve as our protection and provision. We are free to choose God and his way, yet he will not force us. And he is not responsible for the choices we make.

Responsible *To*

This doesn't mean God doesn't feel a sense of responsibility about his creation. As in our example, he does take responsibility (not for us, not for our choices), but that responsibility is *to* us:

- He takes the initiative to *accept* us for who we are and, in fact, sent Christ to "die for us when we were still sinners" (Romans 5:8). This gives us a sense of security.

- He also makes himself *available* to us. He said, "I am with you always, even to the end of the age" (Matthew 28:18). This gives us a sense of importance.

- He expresses *appreciation* to us. To those who are faithful he will say, "Well done, my good and faithful servant" (Matthew 25:23). Feeling appreciated gives us a sense of significance.

- He *affirms* us by identifying with what we go through. As Scripture says, our High Priest Jesus "understands our weaknesses, for he faced all of the same testings we do, yet he did not sin" (Hebrews 4:15). Feeling affirmed gives us a sense of authenticity.

- He makes us *accountable* for what we do or don't do. As Paul stated, "Each of us will give a personal account to God" (Romans 14:12). Feeling accountable gives us a sense of responsibility.

Following God's example, we too can give our kids a sense of security, importance, significance, authenticity, and responsibility when we are responsible *to* them rather than *for* them.

Being Responsible to Hold Our Kids Accountable Gives Them a Sense of Responsibility

Look around. Do you at times see young people who feel entitled—as if the world owes them something? I've noticed it. This sense of entitlement is often fostered in young people when they have not been held accountable for their actions. Consequently they grow up irresponsible, expecting others to do for them.

My son's action in the classroom was wrong. Giving someone "the finger" was unacceptable to me. Sean needed to be held accountable for his action. Because I felt responsible to Sean it took me down a different path than if I had felt responsible for his unacceptable behavior.

If I had felt responsible *for* what Sean did I would have come up with a punishment that would have given me the assurance he wouldn't embarrass me like that again. That of course is a selfish approach, because I would be making the issue about me and how I looked to the school and my community. That approach has little to do with the character building of my son.

In the last chapter I talked about a loving dad, who puts rules within the context of a loving relationship. Well, a loving dad will also put accountability and discipline within the context of a loving relationship. The writer of Hebrews reminds us that "God's discipline is always good for us, so that we might share in his holiness" (Hebrews 12:10). God disciplines us with a purpose—it is to lead us to become more like him. That is certainly for our good, because we were designed to live out his image, which fulfills our purpose and gives us meaning and joy in life. When we hold our kids accountable for their benefit, not ours, it too fulfills their sense of purpose and reinforces their sense of responsibility.

I confess, however, I wasn't a natural at disciplining my kids within the context of relationships. Kelly would do something wrong and I was apt to ground her for six months when two nights would have been more appropriate. It was Dottie who helped me understand the purpose of discipline—that it was to teach responsibility rather than learn how to survive a "prison sentence."

When Dottie and I found out about Sean's "one-finger salute" incident, we sat down and talked about it. We of course did this without his observing or hearing our conversation. Talking things out beforehand with Dottie made a huge difference for me. I was able to vent any unhealthy attitudes or emotions. We have been an excellent balance for each other. Dottie toned me down, and I helped reinforce her fortitude. I needed a more measured response, and Dottie needed more backbone. Our differing strengths offset our separate weaknesses and consequently we parented more effectively.

We sat down with Sean and without heated emotion tried to discover why he had done what he did. You can't always determine why your kids do what they do, but when you can it helps both them and you. It was quite clear Sean had done what he did because he wanted to "earn" the friendship of his soccer teammates. Wanting to win friends is noble, but how he went about it was less than noble. I tried to help him understand that.

Helping Sean understand why his actions were inappropriate was a good thing, but it wasn't necessary in order to hold him accountable for what he did. He needed accountability in his life whether or not he understood why he had disrespected his teacher. But we did get through to him. I'll let him tell you how it worked out. He was in his thirties when he wrote this:

> My parents didn't ground me, deny me a meal or two, or make me go to my room. They sat me down and calmly probed to figure out what I did and why I did it. They both led me to see how disrespectful my actions were to my teacher.
>
> Acknowledging my wrong wasn't such a big deal. But what they said I needed to do was. They told me I needed to apologize to Mrs. Carlson in front of the entire class and also apologize to the class. My dad told me he would go with me if I wanted him to. I said I could do it on my own. It was a humiliating experience. But I learned I was responsible for my actions.
>
> And there was a bonus. My soccer teammates thought my apology was the gutsiest thing they had ever seen. They became my friends after that.

Being Responsible to Accept Our Kids for Who They Are Gives Them a Sense of Security

"My kids won't listen to me, Josh," the dad said while shaking his head slightly. "I really don't get mad at them. I even try to reason with them and let them know I have to hold them accountable for what they do, for their own good. But they seem to resist it. What do I do?"

Like this dad, many of us start off with holding our kids accountable. It seems like rule-keeping should be the first order of business. Enforcing the rules, establishing guidelines, and holding kids accountable seems so important. The reality is that before we establish any accountability we must first lay a foundation of acceptance. Acceptance is the cornerstone of a relationship. Accountability must be firmly planted within the context of an accepting relationship.

Your kids feel accepted when they emotionally feel and know

that no matter how badly they fail or foul things up, their dad loves them anyway.

When children sense true acceptance from their dad, they feel *secure.* They know they are valued and that they have worth that is not determined by how well they perform. They feel safe and secure in the relationship because they are accepted for who they are. Most dads will agree that this is the ideal they aim for, and many believe they are hitting their target. In reality, however, they often offer performance-based (conditional) acceptance to their kids.

In other words, as long as the kids are "good" (perform correctly), their dad accepts them. But if children make mistakes, fail, or get bratty or unreasonable, that acceptance disappears, at least temporarily. Dads can withdraw their acceptance very subtly, without even realizing it, but the child senses it in a heartbeat. To counter performance-based acceptance, we dads must focus on the person, not the performance.

Katie was a great little soccer player, even at the young age of six. After warming up for one of her most important games of the season, she came running off the field and said, "Daddy, if I score a goal, will you give me a dollar?"

"Sure," I answered with a smile.

"Wow!" Katie said. To a six-year-old, a dollar a goal sounds like a multiyear NBA contract.

"Wait a minute," I said, grabbing her before she ran off to join her team. "Even if you don't score a goal, I'll still give you a dollar."

"You will?"

"Yes, I will."

"Wow!" Katie said again as she prepared to scamper off to start the game.

"Wait a minute," I said. "Do you know why?"

My six-year-old stopped and turned around. For at least three years I'd been trying to help her understand what unconditional acceptance is all about, and none of it seemed to mean very much.

But at that moment, she turned, looked at me, and said, "Yeah, it doesn't matter if I'm a good soccer player or not. You love me anyway!"

My daughter couldn't have said anything at that moment to give me more joy. I don't even remember if Katie scored a goal in that game or not. It didn't matter. What did matter was that she knew I loved her regardless of her performance. Our kids need to know we love them as persons regardless of their performance.

How Do You Separate a Person's Actions from Your Acceptance?

Accepting a person for who he or she is regardless of performance is often difficult. I've had fathers come to me and say, "I really want my son to feel I accept him unconditionally, but it's tough when I can't approve of the way he's living."

Many dads get approval and acceptance confused. They can't seem to separate a person's wrong actions from accepting the person. Wrong action seems to cancel out unconditional acceptance. But there is a way to let your kids know they are truly accepted regardless of how they act. The key is to understand how God accepts each of us.

God is holy and "cannot allow sin in any form" (Habakkuk 1:13 NLT). But he "showed his great love for us by sending Christ to die for us while we were still sinners" (Romans 5:8). The truth is God hates sin, yet he accepts us as sinners without any condition. Remember he didn't love you or me nor did he send his Son to die for us upon the condition that we accept his sacrifice for our sin. Jesus died for us "while we were still sinners."

The idea of accepting someone whose actions you can't approve of is often difficult. But understanding how God does it gives us a model of how we can do it. You see, he does find the sinful actions of a person troubling. What is not troubling to him is the person. God is able to separate what a person does from what he or she is.

We make a mistake when we lump what a person does with who that person is. God doesn't do that. It's true we are sinners by birth and his "eyes are too pure to look on evil" and he "cannot tolerate wrongdoing" (Habakkuk 1:13 NIV). But he does accept us because we are his lost children created in his image. He makes a distinction between our "essence" created in his likeness and image and our "nature," which has been infected because of sin.

The core of who we are—the essence of our God-like image—is who and what God accepts. What he cannot accept is our sin, which has infected our nature. It is our sin that separates us from him. Scripture says that "your iniquities have separated you from your God" (Isaiah 59:2 NIV). There is a clear distinction between who we are and what we do. If this weren't true, God could not separate our sins from us and throw them into the depths of his ocean of forgiveness. "He has removed our sins as far from us," David said, "as the east is from the west" (Psalm 103:12). Which is like saying, "Your sins are removed as far as eternity extends." And how can he say this? Because "the LORD is like a father to his children, tender and compassionate to those who fear [respect] him" (Psalm 103:13).

Because of who we are, God's lost children whom he loves and accepts, he can separate our identity from our performance. Because we were molded in his image he "will have compassion on us. You [God] will trample our sins under your feet and throw them into the depths of the ocean!" (Micah 7: 19).

You and I can and must do the same thing with our children if they are to feel secure in our love for them. We must separate their bad behavior from who they are—our very own sons or daughters. Sure, their actions may be appalling. And we can grieve over the realization that their sin may cause them pain and suffering. But they are still our children and we need to accept them as such unconditionally. God accepts you and me that way. He can empower us to accept our kids that way too.

The apostle Paul says, "Accept each other just as Christ has accepted you" (Romans 15:7). Jesus didn't wait until people trusted in him before accepting them. Without condition he accepted them as his lost children in need of him.

The Samaritan woman is a clear example of Jesus' unconditional acceptance. This woman who Jesus met at the well had three strikes against her socially: She was a woman, inferior to men in that culture; she was a Samaritan, despised by the Jews; and her lifestyle was immoral because she was living with a man who was not her husband. What must have amazed this woman was how Jesus accepted her. She must have wondered why he, a man and a Jew, would be so accepting of her. Through the course of the conversation the woman could easily have thought,

- *I am a woman and he is a man. And he can see I'm the kind of woman that strange men have no business talking to. Why is he talking to me?*

- *He is a Jew, and Jews despise us Samaritans. What's wrong with him?*

- *I am an adulterer, which makes it near impossible for even a decent man to interact with me, let alone a man who seems to be a prophet. What is going on here?*

This Samaritan woman had never encountered such a man—one who was so receptive, so open to her, so welcoming. She knew Jesus had no cause to accept her the way he did. Being an immoral woman she was rejected by most. She must have felt alienated and alone. But despite all that, this extraordinary man received her with open arms.

His acceptance didn't mean he condoned her adultery; he did not. Yet he didn't show disappointment in who she was either. He still saw the beauty, the potential, and the innate worth and dignity his Father had infused into every human by virtue of creation, and he loved her for who she was. Jesus didn't condemn her either. Even though she wasn't worshipping correctly he loved her enough to tell her the truth. It is also clear that Jesus' acceptance of her had nothing to do with her own actions. Nothing she could say or do or not say or not do would have caused the Messiah to accept her as he did, to show her such respect, and let her know she was so welcome in his presence. He accepted her as she was and gave her a vision of who she could be. That is the nature of Jesus' kind of acceptance. [2]

Doesn't that kind of acceptance give you a sense of security? When you accept your kids that way it gives them security too. They will feel that no matter what they do or don't do you will always be the dad who loves them. When they feel accepted like that you might hear them quoting a variation of Romans 8: "I am convinced that nothing can ever separate me from my Dad's love" (Romans 8:38 AKV—Accepted Kids Version).

That's the kind of relationship that will prompt them to open up and share their concerns and struggles, their questions and fears, and their hopes and dreams. Accept your child for who he or she is and you will have a child who feels safe enough to share his or her heart with you. Being responsible to accept your kids for who they are gives them a sense of security.

4

I Will Do My Best to Be Responsible *to* My Kids Rather Than *for* Them

Second Part

The pressure was on. The book deadline was fast approaching, and I needed to focus on writing and editing. Although the memory of this experience takes me back over 30 years, I recall it vividly. I was right in the middle of editing a chapter when two-year-old Sean wandered in.

"Want to play, Daddy?" he chirped expectantly.

As an "experienced" parent (we had already been through the two-year-old stage with Kelly), I should have realized that Sean really only wanted a hug, a pat, and a minute or two to show me the new ball he was carrying. But I was working on an important chapter and felt I didn't have even two minutes to spare.

"Son, how about a little later?" I replied. "I'm right in the middle of a chapter."

Sean didn't know what a chapter was, but he got the message. Daddy was too busy, and he'd have to leave now. He trotted off without complaining, and I returned to my manuscript. But my relief was short-lived. Dottie soon came in and sat down for a "little chat."

She began, "Honey, Sean just told me you were too busy to play with him. I know that this book is important, but I'd like to point something out."

"What is that?" I asked rather impatiently, because now my wife was keeping me from my all-important project.

"Josh, I think you have to realize you are always going to have writing to do, and you are always going to have deadlines. Your whole life will be researching and doing projects. But you're not always going to have a two-year-old son who wants to sit on your lap and ask you questions and show you his new ball."

"I think I hear what you're saying," I said, "and you make a lot of sense as usual. But right now I've got to finish this chapter."

"All right, Josh," she said. "But think about it. You know, if we spend time with our kids now, they will spend time with us later."

I did think about it, and the more I thought, the more Dottie's gentle words were like a knife slicing me to the core. She was right. I would always have deadlines to meet, contracts to fulfill, phone calls to answer, people to see, and trips to take. But my children would only be children for a short time. Soon the years would sweep by. Would I have any more time for them next year than I did this year?

I knew what the answer would be if I didn't change my ways. Quietly, without any big speeches or fanfare, I made a decision. Ever since, I have tried to place my children ahead of my contracts, deadlines, and the clamor of a world that wants me to get back to them ASAP. For more than 30 years, I have done my best to make my family my number-one priority.

Being Responsible to Make Time for Our Kids Gives Them a Sense of Importance

You can give your kids an American Girl doll, a smartphone, a video-game player, new clothes—you name it—but nothing will be more valuable to them than your time. Kids spell love T-I-M-E.

When you make yourself available to your kids it tells them they are important.

Let's say you're a good personal friend of the top executive at the company you work at—he's your boss. One Friday, you need to see him on short notice. So you go to his office and ask his assistant if you could talk to him for just a few minutes. The assistant tells you, "I'm sorry, but he's totally booked up until next Tuesday. You'll have to come back."

Because you really need to see him now, you tell the assistant, "Look, I won't take much of his time. Please just tell him it's me and I need to see him. It will only take a minute." And then suppose the secretary calls your boss and tells him you're there. She mentions your name, but all she hears back is, "Have him e-mail me what it's about—I'm really too busy to see him right now. Have him come back next Tuesday."

Now, how would you feel? Sure, you can understand the need to meet deadlines and that there's only so much a person can fit in a day. But you would still most likely feel a little shut out and think, *Obviously I'm not important enough to my boss that he wants to see me.*

That's how our kids feel when we tell them the equivalent of "Sorry, come back next Tuesday." It takes time and effort to make your kids feel important. And your time is what your kids need.

Dads need to give time to their kids, but it's a certain kind of time that's important. Simply hanging around your kids or having them follow you around isn't the point. What's important is that you enter their world and demonstrate you are interested in who they are and what they're involved in.

I remember one dad lamenting to me that spending time with his son didn't work. "He just moped around all day," he said. "My boy didn't seem to enjoy himself at all."

"What did you do with him?" I asked. "I took him golfing with me." "Does your boy like to golf?" I inquired. "No he doesn't, but I do," he replied.

Making yourself available to your kids is about being involved in their lives and being interested in their world. You can't necessarily do that every time you are with your kids, but the more you identify with their world, the more they will connect with you.

I've had dads tell me this: "Josh, my schedule is just too packed to spend the *quantity* of time I want with my kids, so what I focus on is a *quality* time with them." One of the biggest myths going today is the myth of "quality time." Of course we all want quality moments with our kids. But you don't get quality time by appointment or on some kind of tight schedule. You get quality moments by spending larger quantities of time with them. Out of the quantity comes the quality. We must have both!

Another myth we fall victim to is the one that says, "It's the big moments that count." You might call them the Disney World experiences—those major excursions that take all day—even all week—and usually cost a lot of money. These "big moments" might include trips to an amusement park, a movie theater, or the zoo, a ski trip, or an ocean cruise. I used to believe that it was the big moments that counted with my kids, so I would haul them off someplace to show them a good time. Finally, Dottie got through to me in her quiet but laser-accurate way: "Honey, it's not the big times they're going to remember. It's the consistent small moments that will mold them. That's what they are really going to remember."

She's right. Put Disney World experiences on your schedule from time to time. Big moments are necessary, but they can never replace the consistent little moments of being with them. Do your best to be responsible to make time for your kids and you will give them a sense that they are important.

Being Responsible to Express Appreciation to Your Kids Gives Them a Sense of Significance

Accepting a child for who he or she is without condition is foundational for a secure relationship. Expressing appreciation to a child is the necessary building block that gives him or her a sense of significance.

Unconditionally accepting your kids tells them that their *being* matters. Expressing your appreciation to them says that their *doing* matters too. It allows them to feel that they are valued and that their accomplishments do make a difference to their dad. It conveys the idea, "Hey, I'm worth something to him! My dad likes having me around—and he's proud of me!"

Appreciation is a solidly biblical principle. When Jesus was baptized, his heavenly Father expressed appreciation by saying, "This is my dearly beloved Son, who brings me great joy" (Matthew 3:17). What was the heavenly Father doing? He was expressing appreciation to and for his Son. If God the Father took time to express appreciation for his Son in front of the watching world, we should take time to appreciate our sons and daughters at home or in public.

Unfortunately, a lot of kids grow up without receiving appreciation and praise. They eventually learn to become suspicious of compliments, thinking that perhaps they are being set up. Consider trying this exercise with your kids. Stop one of them and say, "Hey, I need to talk to you."

"Yeah, is there something wrong?" he or she may reply.

Then say, "No, I just want to tell you what a great job you did!" And then spell out what that great job was.

You will notice that the more you praise your kids for what they are doing right, the less you have to criticize and discipline them for doing something wrong. That's because praise becomes a motivator for proper behavior.

In my early years as a dad, my approach tended toward catching my kids doing something wrong and then disciplining them for their misbehavior. As a father, I thought I had an absolute obligation to correct practically everything they did. For example, when I learned that Kelly had gotten straight A's on her report card, I wouldn't interrupt my work to tell her "Great job!" And by dinnertime I might have forgotten about it. But if I heard that she had clobbered her sister I would have said indignantly, "Young lady, come in here right now. I need to talk to you."

I could give you countless examples of my focusing on negative behavior with my kids in those early days. What I didn't realize was that I was teaching them something I didn't want to communicate at all: "The fastest way to get Dad's attention is to do something wrong." Today as I talk to young people across the country, I estimate that 15 out of 20 kids tell me that is exactly how it is at their house. They can get the attention of dad and other adults much faster if they do something wrong.

In the mid-'80s, when my kids were all under 11 years old, God spoke to me through—of all things—a book entitled *The One Minute Manager.* In that book, authors Kenneth Blanchard and Spencer Johnson contended that managers could help their employees set and reach business goals if they applied a principle of catching them doing something right and showing appreciation for their efforts. It was easy to apply the message to my parenting. Instead of seeing my job as a matter of catching my kids doing something wrong and correcting them, I learned how to relate to my kids differently. My new motto was, *Try to catch my kids doing something right and praise them for it.* This didn't mean I wasn't going to deal with their misbehavior—it simply meant I was going to outweigh any disciplining efforts many times over by catching them doing something right and praising them for it.

It's funny how a little phrase like that can bring a concept or principle to life. I was sold on giving my kids complete acceptance, but I had been struggling with learning how to appreciate them. One side of me had been trying to accept my children, and the other side had been trying to correct them for doing things wrong. It was no wonder that I often felt a little schizophrenic! But all that changed when I turned the emphasis upside down. Instead of concentrating on what they were doing *wrong,* I started making a conscious effort to look for what they were doing *right*. My new goal was to find at least two things about each child that I could appreciate every day and then to be sure to compliment him or her on what I saw.

I'm not sure my kids noticed a change overnight, but I know I did. My whole perspective changed. When I saw Kelly studying, I would try to say, "Honey, I appreciate the way you study." When I saw Sean taking out the trash, I would try to stop him and say, "Sean, thanks for remembering to take out the trash." And when I caught Katie picking up her toys, I would try to say, "Katie, Daddy really appreciates how you take care of your toys." When Heather was helping her mom clean, I would try to comment, "Heather, you are such a help to Mommy. Thank you for being so helpful."

Try this. Gather your family together in the same general area and stand in the middle of all of them for an "appreciation session." Think of at least one thing about each young person and share it out loud. This exercise will help remind you of just how much you have to be thankful for in your kids, and it will keep you primed for saying appreciative things at the proper time. You see, it isn't a matter of not being able to find things to appreciate about your kids; it's about disciplining yourself to *speak up and tell your kids what you see*—to give them honest praise for their effort.

I talk to dads who have the concept of fathering I used to have, and they say, "Well, kids are *supposed* to do certain things. Why should they be praised for something as ordinary as taking out the trash?" My response is, "Why not? How do you feel when you are praised for doing your job?" Anyone loves to hear the boss say, "I appreciate the way you handled that project." In the same way, your kids crave to be appreciated for even simple and expected chores. For example, you can say things like

- "Thank you for getting your homework done on time."
- "I appreciate it when you take your dirty dishes to the sink after we eat."

- "Thank you for putting the car in the garage for me without being asked."
- "I appreciate you for spending time with your little sister when you wanted to be out with your friends."
- "Thanks for mowing the lawn—you did a great job."

Having said all this about appreciation, here is a word of caution: unless your kids are absolutely convinced that you accept them for who they are, your praise and appreciation can become manipulative. Appreciation without acceptance may prompt your child to relate to you on a performance basis, thinking, *If I do a good job…if I get A's…if I score a goal…then my dad will love me.* Living on a performance basis will tend to produce feelings of false guilt in your kids.

That's why you need to be sure your kids first feel accepted *then* appreciated. For example, when your kids get their report cards, sit down with them and talk about what they achieved. Assure them that, while you appreciate their efforts to earn good grades, you always want them to know, "Even if you didn't get A's, I would love you just as much and accept you just the same."

Admittedly, there is a fine line to walk here. But the best way to walk that line is to keep the acceptance of your kids as the foundation and build from that with appreciation. Make your children feel so secure and so accepted for who they are that they will know you will love them whether they succeed or not. In other words, *Appreciate your child's efforts more than your child's accomplishments, and appreciate your kids' worth as God's creation even more than your kids' efforts.* Do your best to be responsible to express appreciation to your kids and they will gain a sense of significance.

Being Responsible to Affirm Your Kids Gives Them a Sense of Authenticity

To affirm someone is to validate him or her, or to confirm what he or she feels. When we identify with what our kids feel we tell them they are real individuals with valid feelings. When we affirm their feelings of excitement or disappointment, we let them know they are understood for who they really are—authentic human beings.

What do you do when your child gets angry? You may be quick to jump all over them with something like "Get a grip; you're way out of line here!" Or when your kids get giddy and noisy over a happy event, you may be less concerned about their joy than you are about their being too loud or too careless in their excitement. I've found if a dad moves in to affirm his kids' feelings, he confirms that they are real people who are understood.

"Wait a minute, Josh," you may interject. "You can't just let kids vent their feelings all over everybody else. Somebody might get hurt." I agree. I'm talking about *affirming* our kids' feelings, not giving them permission to *vent* their feelings any way they like. There's a big difference. Pure emotions are neither right nor wrong. But how a person *expresses* those emotions can either be right or wrong. The apostle Paul says, "In your anger do not sin" (Ephesians 4:26 NIV). He's not saying it is sinful to be angry; he's warning us not to express our anger in a sinful way. With our kids, it is okay to affirm what they are feeling while at the same time correcting them if they express those feelings in a wrong way.

So how do we affirm our kids' feelings so they sense they are understood? How do we emotionally connect with our kids as they tumble through the highs and lows of their emotions? Scripture tells us, "When others are happy, be happy with them. If they are sad, share their sorrow" (Romans 12:15 NLT).

While the instruction of Romans 12 is profoundly simple, it is not always that easy. You may be tempted to deal with your kids' behavior or try to fix their problem before affirming their feelings. Resist that temptation. Affirm your children's feelings by feeling with them before you deal with any resulting behavior. If your son is excited over making the team, convey that you are excited with him and for him. If your daughter is disappointed over losing a friend, let her know that you are disappointed with her and for her. If she's upset over a false rumor that was started by a "friend," you need to share how sad you are that she hurts. And when you do, your child will feel like a real, authentic person who is being understood—and that will increase the emotional attachment between you and your child.

Like I said, this may seem simple—but I've found it difficult to put into practice myself. I had to work at it; you may need to work on it too. Consider these situations:

- Arriving home from an evening out, your 17-year-old son confesses that he got into a fender-bender with the family car. How do you respond?

- Your 14-year-old daughter, a B-plus student, brings home a report card with three Cs and a D. What will you say to her?

- Your athletic high-school daughter calls you in tears and says she has been cut from the volleyball team by a coach who doesn't like her. What will your first words be?

- Your son comes home with cuts and scratches on his face, admitting that he got into a fight with another boy. How will you handle it?

These trying situations, and countless others like them, reflect life as usual in the activity of raising your family. Kids make mistakes. Kids have problems. Kids get hurt. Kids get into trouble. Kids are victimized by other kids—even by adults. Sometimes these incidents are genuine crises: a life-threatening disease or injury, the breakup of a serious relationship, the death of a friend or relative, and so on. But most of the time they are the relatively minor disappointments, losses, conflicts, and hurts of everyday life.

The critical question is, how do you deal with your kids in the day-to-day difficulties of life? If your first response is to enforce the rules, correct the behavior, or fix the problem, there is no way your

kids are going to feel understood. The best thing to do is to first identify with what they are feeling and let them know you feel sad with
them.

I remember the first time I got a handle on the truth of Romans
12:15. It happened with Dottie. Previously when she had come to
me with a problem she was struggling with, especially one that had
caused her hurt, I would try to fix it. I wouldn't address her pain—
rather I would address the problem that *caused* the pain.

One day she came home from a meeting at school very hurt over
what some mothers had said about one of our kids. In the past when
she shared a problem like that with me, I would leap on the situation
and say something like, "Honey, don't let it get to you. Here's what
you need to do." Then I would outline a plan to fix the problem. It
may have been a good plan, but it didn't address the pain Dottie felt
at the moment. But on this particular occasion, I finally got it right.
I simply put my arms around her and said, "Honey, I'm so sorry that
you had to hear those words, and I hurt for you." That was it—no
fix-it plan, no corrective measures outlined, just a heartfelt expression that identified with her pain.

Amazingly, it worked. Dottie felt affirmed and understood, and
that was all she needed at the moment. A few days later she came
back to me and asked what I thought she could do to address those
critical comments about the family member. My fix-it plan was then
welcomed.

We don't have to understand exactly what our kids or even our
wives are going through in order to affirm them. You can affirm
someone even when you can't fully appreciate the pain they are going
through. In fact it is counterproductive to indicate you "understand"
their hurt rather than simply hurting that they hurt.

A friend of mine found this out the hard way. Once when his wife
was at a very low point emotionally, he, in an effort to help her, said,
"Honey, I know just what you're going through." She snapped back
angrily, "No, you don't! How dare you say you know what I'm going

through?" My friend was speechless, but his wife was right. To share in a person's difficulty doesn't mean that we necessarily know what he or she is going through. We can't always participate in another person's unique experience—especially that of our kids. Affirming our kids means that because we know they are hurting, we *hurt* with them. It means we identify with the one we love who is feeling the pain. My friend should have said, "Honey, what you're going through must be tough, and I want you to know that I hurt because you hurt."

That's how we can identify with our kids' difficulties and pain without giving the impression that we know exactly how they feel—which they know is not true. Use words similar to these when your kids are struggling and hurting. "What you're going through must really hurt you, and I want to let you know that I hurt with you. And I'll be here for you." Your kids will not only feel your comfort but they will also experience God's comfort. Paul tells us that "God is our merciful Father and the source of all comfort. He comforts us in all our troubles so that we can comfort others. When others are troubled, we will be able to give them the same comfort God has given us" (2 Corinthians 1:3-4 NLT). Comfort happens when we follow God's instructions in Romans 12 to "share their sorrow."

Of course we can also affirm our kids and give them a sense of authenticity when we follow the instructions of the first part of Romans 12:15: "Be happy with those who are happy." When one of your kids gets excited about something, join in with him or her and say something like: "I'm so happy for you!"; "This is so great!"; "I'm so excited that this happened to you!"; "You have every right to be thrilled—I am too!"; and so on. You can also affirm their feelings through what you do. Happy times sometimes call for celebrations and gifts, but they don't have to be extravagant. Take your young child out for lunch, dinner, or ice cream; bring him or her a new CD; allow a special privilege; or send an encouraging text. You may not be as excited as your kids are, but if you mirror their joys by being happy with them, they will feel validated, and you will solidify the loving bond between you.

Making a commitment to do your best to be responsible *to* your kids rather than *for* them is critically important:

- *Accept* them for who they are and you will give them a sense of security.

- Make yourself *available* and enter their world and they will gain a sense of importance.

- Express *appreciation* and they will enjoy a sense of significance.

- *Affirm* them by identifying with them in their happiness and sadness and you will give them a sense of authenticity.

- And hold them *accountable* for their actions and you will gift them with a sense of responsibility.

5

COMMITMENT #3

I Will Do My Best to Be an Authentic Model

He pulled the car to the side of the road. He stepped out and motioned to the farmer working on his tractor. "Excuse me," the man called. "Could you tell me how to get to Dover?"

"Sure," the farmer responded, "it's only four miles from here. Take this road for about a mile and you'll come to a crossroad. Make a left and that will take you directly into Dover." The man thanked the farmer as he climbed back into his car.

As the car reached the crossroad, the man turned right. His wife, who was riding with him, said, "Henry, the farmer said to take a left—you just turned right."

"I know, dear," the man replied, "but did you notice when he said left he actually motioned right? Well, I've long learned that when a person's words contradict their actions, what they do is what they mean." The man and his wife turned right and drove straight to Dover.

That's an old story but it illustrates this point: we may try to teach our kids the right things by telling them what to do and think, but how we live our lives before them is what we are actually teaching them.

Seeing Is Believing

Your kids are growing up in a culture that says that you can tell if something is true by whether or not it works. That may be faulty thinking (because actually we know that something is true if it is right), but the point is this generation wants to see things working before they embrace them. To them, seeing is believing.

You can use that to your advantage by being a model before your kids. As they see you live a life of faithfulness, honesty, mercy, respect of others, fairness, justice, compassion, self-control, and so on, they will be far more apt to embrace those values for themselves. Being a role model to your kids is important, but being an *authentic* model is even more important. Because—let's face it—none of us are perfect, but all of us can be real.

"Where do you guys want to eat?" I asked. Speaking all at once each of my kids yelled out their own favorite local fast-food restaurant. It was almost unanimous. Everyone but Kelly chose the same place. We jumped in the car and as we pulled out of the driveway Kelly stated disparagingly, "I can't believe we're going to that garbage can again!"

I quickly responded. "Kelly, I don't appreciate your tone or your language." I told her it wasn't nice to dump on the place her brother and sisters wanted to go to just because she didn't like it. In a more respectful tone she cited her reasons for objecting, so we compromised. We agreed to drop off Sean, Katie, and Heather at the "objectionable" restaurant, and Dottie and I would take Kelly to her choice. As I pulled up to the restaurant to drop off our three kids I said, "Everyone out for the gag bag."

The younger kids didn't even hear my sarcastic remark—they were too excited about the french fries and burgers they were planning to order. As we pulled away for Kelly's choice of restaurant, she said, "Dad, you just did what you told me was wrong—what's the difference between calling a place a garbage can or a gag bag?"

I could have said to Kelly, "The big difference, young lady, is that I'm the parent here and you're the child—I'm the one doing the correcting and you're the one being corrected." But I didn't. Kelly had me cold, and I knew it. We were heading out for dinner, but I was going to have my own words for hors d'oeuvres. I swallowed hard and thanked Kelly for pointing out my inconsistency and the fact I was being hypocritical—telling her to do one thing and me doing the other. I apologized.

I wasn't a perfect model, but I was an authentic one. It's true—as dads we should model all the virtues of godliness. But the reality is, we are human and we blow it. We need to face up to our shortcomings, humble ourselves, and seek forgiveness. That makes us authentic models, the kind from which our kids can actually learn how to make amends when they mess up.

Who's Accountable to Whom?

Some would say that you show weakness when you confess your failures to your kids. If you let your kids "correct" you, they say, it will encourage them to disrespect you. Much of this thinking comes from the autocratic parent who demands respect. I prefer to *earn* respect by demonstrating that my kids are highly respected themselves and have insights that are helpful to me.

Another reason some feel you shouldn't be vulnerable with your kids is a misguided view of leadership. There are those who feel that God has set the father up as the "CEO of the home," "the absolute ruler of his family," and "the king of the castle." They imply then that the dad is the model teacher with his kids being his submissive students. In some cases this kind of dad may even look upon his own wife as a submissive student as well.

Jesus, however, made it clear to his disciples what real leadership was all about. They too had a misconception about being the "head" of something or having "authority" over people. Let's look at Jesus' exposé of bad leadership and explanation of the good kind. He said,

> In this world the kings and great men lord it over their
> people, yet they are called "friends of the people." But
> among you it will be different. Those who are the greatest

among you should take the lowest rank, and the leader
should be like a servant. Who is more important, the
one who sits at the table or the one who serves? The one
who sits at the table, of course. But not here! For I am
among you as one who serves (Luke 22:25-27).

Jesus was espousing a whole new concept of authority and leadership. The common view was that people submit to and serve leaders and those in authority. But Jesus' view was that leaders are to serve. He shared this revolutionary concept of how to lead during the Passover meal just before he gave his life for the church. John records him getting up from the meal and starting to wash the disciples' feet just as a servant would do. When he finished he said, "Do you understand what I was doing? You call me 'Teacher' and 'Lord,' and you are right, because that's what I am. And since I, your Lord and Teacher, have washed your feet, you ought to wash each other's feet. I have given you an example to follow. Do as I have done to you" (John 13:12-15).

Applying these passages to fathering, how does a dad exercise his authority in his house? If we are to live out Jesus' view on leadership then we are to serve the needs of our families. This concept of having authority as described by Jesus is difficult for many dads to grasp. It turns the idea of leading on its ear, so to speak. How *do you* effectively lead by serving? How *do you* "call the shots" by taking on the "lowest rank"? This approach is confusing if you try to implement it as a hierarchical structure for the family. But it really makes sense when you see this in light of developing an intimate relationship with your kids and spouse.

As a dad you ultimately want a love relationship with your kids in which they willingly allow you to guide and direct them. You want them to be responsive and accountable to you. What better way to teach them accountability than openly demonstrating your accountability to God and in turn making yourself accountable to them?

Now you've really gone off the deep end, McDowell, you might think.

But I tell you there's perhaps no better way to gain your kids' trust, respect, and admiration than to ask them to hold you accountable.

I started first with my wife, Dottie. No one respects and admires me more than the one who shares her life and her love with me—the mother of my children, my sweetheart, my best friend, and the special gift God gave me.

And so I said to her, "Honey, I need your help. Will you hold me accountable as a husband and a father? If I'm on the road too much, tell me. If I'm not meeting your needs or the children's needs, spell it out for me. If I'm not spending enough time with the children or spending enough time with you—I want to know about it."

"Okay, Josh," Dottie replied, just a little bit reluctantly. "I'll tell you, but sometimes it may hurt a little."

"Honey, I know I'm probably going to get defensive sometimes, but when I do, you have the right to tell me that too. I want to hear the truth."

But I wasn't through. When Kelly's seventh birthday rolled around, I put a special note in her birthday card from me:

> Dear Kelly, I sure love you. I count it such a joy to be your dad, but you know, I'm going to need your help this year. I've never been the father of a seven-year-old daughter before. I just want to be the best dad I can be to you. And if you ever feel that I'm not doing right or not being fair, or loving and considerate, please tell me.

When Sean turned seven, I did the same thing with him. In fact, I've done it with all the children. With Katie I said, "I've never been the father of a seven-year-old, blue-eyed blonde before." I did the same with Heather.

Ever since I've asked them for help on being accountable, my wife and kids have become my best counselors. Kelly and Sean, for example, accepted my proposition with enthusiasm. The other kids have put in their two cents' worth on many occasions.

One time Sean and I were walking along the street downtown, when a man stopped to talk to me. Something the man said irritated me and I was rather short with him. As he walked away, Sean remarked, "Dad, you were sorta mean to that man. You didn't talk to him very nicely."

I felt like dying right there on the street. We ran after the man, who was still in sight, and when we caught up with him I stopped him. With my son standing right there with me, I apologized for my rude behavior.

Once when I got back from a trip I was approached by my ten-year-old daughter Katie, who said firmly, "Daddy, you're not being fair to me."

"What do you mean, honey?"

"When you come home from trips, you take Kelly and Sean and Heather out, but not me."

"Really?"

"Yes," my ten-year-old said unflinchingly, and then she added, "Will you take me out for lunch today?"

I was glad Katie had the freedom to hold me accountable by telling me she thought I was being unfair. I thought I had been spending enough time with her, but apparently she hadn't seen it that way, and I was more than happy to oblige her request for lunch. In fact, lunch became a big thing for Katie, and I made it a practice with her during all of her growing-up years.

Understand that making myself accountable to my family wasn't easy for me. I'm not suggesting that Dottie or any of the kids took advantage of my offer to correct me, but they also weren't shy about giving me some "tips."

Sometimes their critiques stung and I got defensive. Every time I became defensive, however, it only caused them to clam up—and there went my greatest source of insight and help. So I learned that although there were moments when I had to choke on my pride as I swallowed it in big hunks, I did it anyway because I knew I couldn't get along without their help.

When we as dads become vulnerable and real and admit we struggle too, we become a powerful model to our kids. The apostle Paul understood about being authentic. He told the Christians in Corinth that he'd had a number of spiritual experiences he could boast about. But he said, "I won't do it. I don't want anyone to think more highly of me than what they can actually see in my life and my message" (2 Corinthians 12:6 NLT).

In using his own life as a model for others to follow, Paul was not lowering the standard of living like Christ. In fact, he told the Corinthians, "Follow my example, as I follow the example of Christ" (1 Corinthians 11:1 NIV). His goal was to be a model of Christlikeness. But he didn't put on a mask or try to position himself as some perfect leader. He was authentic and didn't hide the fact that he had weaknesses. Here is an example of his authenticity:

> To keep me from getting puffed up, I was given a thorn in my flesh, a messenger from Satan to torment me and keep me from getting proud. Three different times I begged the Lord to take it away. Each time he said, "My gracious favor is all you need. My power works best in your weakness." So now I am glad to boast about my weaknesses, so that the power of Christ may work through me...For when I am weak, then I am strong (2 Corinthians 12:7-10 NLT).

The secret to Paul's powerful leadership and positive role model was in recognizing and confessing his weaknesses so the power of Christ could work through him. That's where your power comes from too. Admitting you need help and asking your family to hold you accountable places you in a position for God's power to work through you. He knows your struggles and weaknesses, and fact is, so does your family. Trying to cover it up doesn't hide a thing. It is so much better to own up to your faults and weaknesses and ask for your family's help.

Talk to your wife first. If you haven't already made her your accountability partner, tell her you want to know when you're messing up or when she senses you're about to. Then sit down with your kids and let them know you want to be the best dad you can be, but you need their help. I suggest you do this when your kids are around seven years old. Ask them to hold you accountable. You might consider writing each of your kids a note to "formally" ask them to be your "accountability partner." I think you'll find by doing so you will truly become an authentic model that God will be pleased with.

To help, here are a few ideas you might want to consider if you write out a note with your accountability request.

> Dear (child's name),
>
> I love you. I love your sensitivity, your honesty, your spirit, and caring heart. This note gives you permission to remind me when I'm not sensitive, honest, or caring. I want so much to be a better dad and friend to you.
>
> Forgive me for not giving you more of my time. I really want to be in more of your life. This note gives you permission to remind me when I get too busy with other things. Please use it.
>
> Also forgive me for trying to live my life out in you— playing sports I never played, making grades I never made, being better than I ever was. I'm sorry for my unkind words, my impatience, and harsh spirit. I so want to be kind and loving so that you feel it from me.
>
> This note gives you permission to tell me to back off and give you some space. I need you to help me be a more patient dad. So use this note whenever you need it, and when it wears out, I promise to write you another one.
>
> I love you,
> Dad

Making yourself accountable to your family will draw you closer together so you can better guide your kids down the right path. That is what Commitment #3 is all about—doing your best to be an authentic model.

6

I Will Do My Best to
Explain Who God Is and What He Is Like

Dad, where does God live?" your son asks.

"Well," you respond, "I guess he lives in heaven."

"But we can't see heaven until we die, right?" your daughter chimes in.

"You're right, not until after we die," you confirm.

Your son adds, "And no one has ever actually seen God either, right?"

"Right," you answer, wondering where all this is going.

"Well," your daughter says, scratching her head, "if we can't visit God's home until we die and we can't see him now, then how do we know what he is like or even if he exists at all?"

Now, your kids may never ask it like that, but at some point your kids will have questions about God. And perhaps the most important question you have to answer as a Christian father is, who is God and what is he like? Your kids' eternal destiny and the kind of relationship they have with him largely rests in how they perceive him.

How did you get your own understanding of God? How did you perceive him from childhood and how has that changed in adulthood? As I stated earlier, most of us have acquired our view of God from the dominant authority figure in our lives—generally our father.

If your dad was autocratic—depending on the severity of his approach—you may have viewed God as judgmental. To you he may have been an inspecting God looking to catch you doing something wrong.

If your father was an anything-goes dad you probably grew up feeling that God really wasn't that bothered by what you did or didn't do. And if you had an absentee father you no doubt considered God to be distant.

But if your dad was loving and placed rules within the context of a father-child relationship, then chances are you saw God as a loving being who really cared about you. You probably thought he accepted you for who you were and his commands were for your best interest. If that's the case, your chances of accepting Christ as your Savior and Lord were statistically high.

God designed the family as the prime evangelistic channel to lead children to Christ. You are his best means of sharing the good news that God loves your child and wants an eternal relationship with him or her. The latest statistics show that "83 percent of all Americans make their commitment to Christ between the ages of 4 and 14. Adults age 19 and over have just a 6 percent probability of becoming Christians."[1] Dad, that means you have a golden opportunity to present God to your kids as clearly and accurately as possible. None of us want our kids to believe in an inspecting, permissive, or distant God. We want them to come to know the merciful, loving God of the Scriptures, who is "passionate about his relationship with [us]" (Exodus 34:14 NLT).

At times your kids may ask some tough questions about God. Be ready with answers. It's true that he may be invisible to our physical eyes, but the reality is he is there. And he has given us a clear revelation to know who he is and what he is like.

Unseen yet Clearly There

"All honor and glory to God forever and ever!" the Scripture states. "He is the eternal King, the unseen one who never dies; he alone is

God. Amen" (1 Timothy 1:17). We are unable to see him for a very good reason. He does not exist as a *material* being. "God is Spirit, so those who worship him must worship in spirit and in truth" (John 4:24). That means he is beyond us, on another plane of existence than we humans are.

We are not meant to see God in all his awesome power. He told Moses, "You may not look directly at my face, for no one may see me and live" (Exodus 33:20). His greatness, majesty, and intensity are simply more than the physical bodies of humans can take and still live.

It is important to explain to your kids, beginning at a young age, that God is great and wonderful yet is not limited by existing in a material world. We all are fascinated by those things that are beyond us, even young children. There is a mystery and majesty about God. He is with us and can be "seen" with the heart, not our physical eyes. But just because he is not a material being doesn't mean we can't explain his existence to our kids. He has revealed himself in many ways.

"Long ago God spoke many times and in many ways to our ancestors through the prophets. But now in these final days, he has spoken to us through his Son...The Son reflects God's own glory, and everything about him represents God exactly" (Hebrews 1:1-3 NLT). Jesus is God with skin on. Through the miracle of the Incarnation, God entered our material world and lived, died, and rose again to life so we could have a relationship with him. One of the foundational beliefs of the Christian faith is that God became human: "The Word became human and made his home among us...we have seen his glory, the glory of the Father's one and only Son" (John 1:14). Explain to your kids that God is real and he showed up 2000 years ago because he wanted to have a relationship with us. This was Jesus, whose name is Immanuel, meaning "God with us."

God has also revealed himself through creation. "Through everything God made, they can clearly see his invisible qualities—his eternal power and divine nature" (Romans 1:20). King David said this:

The heavens proclaim the glory of God. The skies display his craftsmanship. Day after day they continue to speak; night after night they make him known. They speak without a sound or word; their voice is never heard. Yet their message has gone throughout the earth, and their words to all the world (Psalm 19:1-4).

The material world we live in tells us it was created by a masterful Intelligent Designer. It is inconceivable to think this world came into being by mere chance. Take opportunities to point out to your kids the intricate details and masterfully designed universe around us as God's wonderful creation. This will help them understand who he is—the creator of all.

Have you ever visited Disneyland or Disney World with your kids? Then you have probably noticed the bed of flowers laid out on a sloping bank near the entrance. The colors, formation, and flower selection form a clear resemblance to Mickey Mouse. No one would attribute that gardening marvel to mere chance. Why? First, flowers of that variety and color don't just grow by chance to form the shape and color of the famous Mickey Mouse. The numerous types of flowers and the intricacy of their placement clearly point to *complexity*. Complexity in this sense is the same as saying it is highly improbable that these flowers randomly grew there or were positioned so exactly by chance.

Second, besides being complex, the floral arrangement is laid out in a very specific manner. Certain flowers make up the eyes, others the nose, and yet others the mouth and the renowned ears. The image exhibits an independently given pattern—it's therefore *specified*.

This combination of complexity (or improbability) and specificity (or independently imposed patterning) is called *specified complexity*. Specified complexity is a marker of intelligence. Like a fingerprint or a signature, specified complexity identifies the activity of an intelligent agent. The huge flower bed at Disney exhibits specified complexity and leads us to believe an intelligent gardener was its cause.

The more specific and complex a thing is, the more it points to an intelligent designer. This world and all that's in it point to the masterful craftsmanship of a real God. Nature movies or a trip to the zoo can serve as great opportunities to marvel with your kids at the amazing design of the world produced by Creator God. You can pose questions like "What does a rose tell us about God and what he likes?" or "Why did God make giraffes with such long necks?" We dads don't necessarily have to know all the detailed scientific answers to things to be in awe at God's miraculous creation and praise him for it.

You can use your children's birthday to marvel about the miracle of birth—another design of our Creator God. The fascinating aspects of our complex bodies are another way to point to him as the master designer. You might remember from high-school biology that the double-helix shape of DNA resembles a twisted ladder. Each rung is a piece of your genetic code, and amazingly, every cell in your body contains a complete DNA blueprint for everything about you. The sequence of those rungs provides the pattern for the production of every building block of your body. Not only that, but within each human being's reproductive cells lies the information that, when combined with genetic information from a mate, adds up to the genetic pattern handed down to your child.

DNA, in other words, is what determines not only *what we are like* but *what our children look like*. Use fascinating information like this to stand in awe of our Creator God. Wonder aloud with your kids—"Where did God come up with the idea of DNA?" "What would it be like to know everything there is to know?" "What does God look like?" "What if he has a favorite color?" "Why does he love us so much?" This exercise isn't meant to reduce God to human size, but rather to help your kids understand a key truth: God is beyond our comprehension on one hand; on the other he is an approachable

God who takes notice even of how many hairs grow on our heads (Matthew 10:30).

There are a number of great resources available to you that can help reinforce to your kids that God is our Master Creator. *Understanding Intelligent Design* by William H. Dembski and Sean McDowell is a good one. Granted, my son is the coauthor. But what can I say—I'm a proud dad! (See more about this resource in the back of this book.)

God has certainly revealed himself by becoming human in the form of Jesus and through creation, but that's not all. He has also revealed himself in our moral consciences (Romans 2:14-15), his Word (2 Timothy 3:16-17), the church (Ephesians 1:23), history (1 Samuel 17:46-47), and through the indwelling of his Holy Spirit in our lives (Romans 8:9-11). God may be beyond us in a material, physical sense, but there is clear evidence he is real and with us today.

Teach Your Kids to Be in Awe of God

There is so much to know about God and everything about him is awesome. As a dad, one of the best things you can do in presenting him to your kids is teach them to be in awe of him. That is another way of saying "teach your kids to fear God."

King Solomon said, "Fear of the LORD is the beginning of wisdom. Knowledge of the Holy One results in understanding" (Proverbs 9:10 NLT). Teach your kids to fear God. I'm not talking about dread or fright, like they might feel about terrorists, poisonous snakes, or tornadoes. God is not to be dreaded. Instead, because he is awesome we are to be in awe of him, respect him, and have a profound awareness of who he is and what he can do.

This kind of fear—being in awe of who God is—is healthy. He told the prophet Jeremiah why the children of Israel were to fear him. "I will put the fear of Me in their hearts so that they will not turn away from Me" (Jeremiah 32:40 NASB). As you instill awe in your kids for who God is, it will draw them to him and help keep them from turning away from him.

There are at least three aspects of God we need to teach our kids. Each of these inspires within us awe—healthy respect and fear—of him that will draw us to him:

- *His infinite characteristics*, for example, speak of his greatness.

- *His holy nature* may seem scary since we as humans are sinful. But the implications of his perfection are extremely relevant to our lives.

- Of course *his relational heart* is supremely meaningful, but even more than you perhaps think.

Let's discover these three aspects of God and how to share them with our kids.

Living in Awe of God's Infinite Characteristics
He Is Eternal

God possesses an infinite life that is without beginning or end—he is eternal. "Have you never heard? Have you never understood? The LORD is the everlasting God, the Creator of all the earth" (Isaiah 40:28). God created time and he involves himself within time, but he exists eternally, outside of time. There was never a moment when he didn't exist, nor will he ever end. His being eternal is something to be in awe of.

Truth is, we have no way of comprehending the eternal. We can't wrap our minds around a being who has never had a beginning or will never have an end. What we grasp clearly is that things run down and have an end. We can relate to a broken toy, a run-down car, a deteriorating body, even death itself. Those things happen in our decaying world. That reality doesn't bring happy thoughts. The point, though, is that God is eternal. He is the solution to the temporal and decaying world. He has come to bring eternal life—a life where nothing wears out, runs down, or dies!

Try this with your kids. While riding in the car play this little game. Ask, "How long will _____ last?" Explore together how long things will last such as your car, the coat you wear, the house you live in, a bird, an elephant, a tree, a bee, and so on. You get the idea. Guess how long things last here on earth. Then ask, "How long will God last?" Make the point that he is eternal.

Talk about the mind-blowing idea of someone never having a beginning or end. Then ask why the lights in God's heavenly home will never go out. Why will his rivers never run dry? Why will the clothes he gives the people who live with him never wear out? Explain the reason is that he plans to give us eternal life. He wants us to live forever with him. Ask one of your kids to read what Jesus said: "I am the resurrection and the life. Anyone who believes in me will live, even after dying. Everyone who lives in me and believes in me will never ever die" (John 11:25-26). Share how you are in awe of God's being eternal and how thankful you are that he offers you and your family life forever in a place that never grows old.

He Is All-Powerful

The Bible reveals a God who is almighty—what is called *omnipotent*. If he wants to do something—anything—he can do it. King David said, "How great is our Lord! His power is absolute" (Psalm 147:5). The Almighty God as Sovereign of the universe has the power to know the future and cause it to happen:

> I am God, and there is none like me. Only I can tell you
> the future before it even happens. Everything I plan will
> come to pass, for I do whatever I wish (Isaiah 46:9-10).

We live in a world with limited natural energy sources. Eventually we will run out of coal, oil, gas, and all fossil fuels. As humans we also have only so much strength and power to do things. It's hard to comprehend the idea of perpetual energy or unlimited power and strength. But that is who God is—a being with absolute power, energy, and strength. He can do anything. As limited, finite humans we need a power source like that.

Here are some questions to ask your kids: "How many miles can you run before you fall over?" "How long can you go without drinking anything?" "How long can you go without eating?" "How long can you go without sleep?"

Then ask questions about God. When does he tire out? Does he need to eat or drink or sleep? Who can defeat him? Can he do anything he wants? Have one of your kids read the verse I mentioned on the previous page: "How great is our Lord! His power is absolute!" (Psalm 147:5). Read what Jeremiah said: "You made the heavens and earth by your strong hand and powerful arm. Nothing is too hard for you!" (Jeremiah 32:17).

That's the kind of God and friend to have—someone who can do anything, anytime. Then ask your kids, "Does this mighty God want to help us?" Have a child read from Psalm 145: "The Lord always keeps his promises; he is gracious in all he does. The Lord helps the fallen and lifts those bent beneath their loads. The eyes of all look to you in hope; you give them their food as they need it. When you open your hand, you satisfy the hunger and thirst of every living thing" (Psalm 145:13-16). Explain to your kids how you are in awe of a God who is all-powerful. Let them know it's not just that you are blown away at his unlimited abilities, but that he wants to give you his strength when you need it. Share how you want to let him change you to be more patient, kind, gentle, loving, and so on. Let them know how thankful you are that he is all-powerful.

He Is Everywhere-Present

God's person has no limits, no boundaries—which is why we say he is *omnipresent*: present everywhere. Again, as finite beings we cannot imagine a being who can be everywhere-present within our universe of time and space. "'Am I a God who is only close at hand?' says the LORD. 'No, I am far away at the same time. Can anyone hide from me in a secret place? Am I not everywhere in all the heavens and earth?' says the LORD" (Jeremiah 23:23-24).

At first God's omnipresence may seem a little scary because he sees everything we do, when we do it. That means he sees the good and the bad in our lives. The good thing, however, is that we are never left alone. No matter where we are or what has happened to us or what we have done—God is there for us. That is something to be in awe of.

Here's a story with some questions to ask your kids. Let's say you were on vacation at your all-time favorite place. Your best friend back home texted you and said he or she really needs your help, like in a real emergency. So you need to go right away. But you don't want to leave your vacation because you're having a great time. How do you solve the problem?

After a little discussion, tell your kids, "Now let's say you have miraculous powers. How could you use your powers to stay on vacation and still help your friend at the same time?"

The solution of course is having the power to be in more than one place at a time—a characteristic God possesses. Ask one of your kids to read Jeremiah 23:23-24. Then ask, "What's the benefit to us that God is everywhere at the same time?" Lead your kids to the realization that he can be there for everyone when they need him most. He is not limited by time and space. That is why Jesus could say, "Be sure of this: I am with you always, even to the end of the age" (Matthew 28:20). God is everywhere-present—and that means we are never truly alone. That is something to be in awe of.

He Knows All

God has infinite knowledge. He knows everything past, present, and future—what is called *omniscient*. In a passage we read earlier, he declares, "I am God, and there is none like me. Only I can tell you the future before it even happens. Everything I plan will come to pass, for I do whatever I wish" (Isaiah 46:9-10). Take everything there is to know within the known universe and that wouldn't even scratch the surface of God's knowledge. But how does his knowledge about everything help us?

Let's say everything is going well right now. However, that doesn't mean that things are going to be okay tomorrow. The unknown is what causes us to worry. Although we humans can't know what is going to happen in the future, we can know someone who holds the future. You and your family can trust in a God who knows the future and says, "Everything I plan will come to pass." There is security in an all-knowing God.

Ask your kids these questions: "Have you ever misspelled a word?" "Can you remember a time you got lost?" "Of all there is to know in the world, how much of it do you know?" Ask one of your kids to read Isaiah 46:9-10 and Psalm 139:1.

Then guide your kids in this direction: How much does God really know? Does he know the past, present, and future? How does our knowing that lead us to put our present and future in his hands?

We can trust in a God who knows everything. We can rely on a God who knows the future and tells us we have a home waiting for us in his heavenly home.

He Does Not Change

By his very nature God can be counted on. He is unchanging—what is called *immutable*. This means he will not waver or lie. He will always do what he says he will do.

> God is not a man, so he does not lie. He is not human, so he does not change his mind. Has he ever spoken and failed to act? Has he ever promised and not carried it through? (Numbers 23:19).

God's being unchanging means he infinitely remains constant, firm, and secure—you can trust whatever he is because he will always be that for all eternity.

Some time ago, I was in South Africa, sharing evidence for the Christian faith with Muslims. In one of my talks, I made a point about the consistency and immutability of God's character. I said that he always acts according to his righteous nature. What he *does* is always consistent with who he is.

After my talk, a young Muslim approached me. "Your concept of God," he said, "is not my concept of Allah. Allah is 'all-powerful.' Allah's 'powers' can allow him to do anything."

"Can Allah lie and cheat?" I asked.

"Sure," he responded. "Allah can do all things. He is not limited like your God. If he wants to love, he loves. If he wants to hate, he hates. Allah is 'all-powerful.'"

"Could Allah punish you for something you did," I asked, "even if it were good?"

"If Allah did not like it, he would punish me."

"Then you don't always know how Allah might respond, do you?"

He thought for a moment. "No," he said. "I don't always know what he would do." He stopped, but added quickly. "But I do know Allah is 'all-powerful.'"

I nodded. "You see, if I served Allah, I would be serving him out of fear. If he exercised the power to do wrong as well as right simply because he desired to, he would be punishing me from his own selfish desires. That would be a dreadful motivation from which to serve him, because I would never know what angered him." He was listening intently, so I continued. "You see, I serve God out of love. His being holy and perfect and almighty is worthy of my fear—my respect. But because I know he is merciful and always acts consistently with his loving nature, I serve him out of love. I always know what angers him and I always know what pleases him because he infinitely remains consistent by his very nature."

I walked away from that conversation even more in awe of the God I serve. He can always be counted on to act lovingly because it's in his unchanging nature do so. One of the things kids want and need is security. And what makes us feel more secure than someone we can count on? Share with your kids that more than anyone in all the world, God is the one they can count on to be there for them and always do right by them. "He remains faithful," Scripture says, "for he cannot deny who he is" (2 Timothy 2:13).

Ask your kids these questions: "Why can't you count on every day being a sunny day?" "Why can't you count on never getting sick?" "Why can't you count on your friends never disappointing you?" "Is there anything or anyone in your life you can always count on no matter what?" Have one of your kids read Numbers 23:19.

Then ask, "Why can we always count on God to be there for us and do right by us?" "How does it make you feel that he can't do anything wrong?" Share with them how much in awe you are that God is absolutely consistent in his loving nature. Tell them that is just one thing that makes him so awesome!

Living in Awe of God's Holy Nature

None of us can come close to grasping the infinite characteristics of God but we know he is eternal, all-powerful, everywhere-present, all-knowing, and never-changing. We are finite beings, yet we are created in his image to relate to him. And perhaps of all the infinite characteristics of God, this last one—his unchanging nature—is the one we can best relate to.

God can be counted on because by his very nature he is holy, perfect, and righteous. Scripture says, "He is the Rock; his deeds are perfect. Everything he does is just and fair. He is a faithful God who does no wrong; how just and upright he is!" (Deuteronomy 32:4).

Scripture reveals a God who is perfectly holy (Isaiah 54:5 and Revelation 4:8), just (Revelation 16:5), and right (Psalm 119:137). This isn't something he *decides* to do. In other words, he doesn't simply decide to do holy, just, and right things; this is something he *is*. And all that is right and holy and just and good is derived from his core nature—his essence. The Scripture says, "Whatever is good and perfect comes down to us from God our Father, who created all the lights in the heavens" (James 1:17).

It is so important that we dads instill this truth into our children. Each of our kids needs to understand that our holy God is pure goodness. All that is perfect and right and beautiful and complete and meaningful and eternally full of contentment, joy, and happiness is because of him and comes from him. His very nature and essence are good. "The LORD is good and does what is right" (Psalm 25:8). He is "the one who is holy and true" (Revelation 3:7). "Holy, holy, holy is the LORD Almighty" (Isaiah 6:3 NIV). "The LORD is righteous in everything he does; he is filled with kindness" (Psalm 145:17). "The LORD is just! He is my rock! There is no evil in him" (Psalm 92:15).

Ask your kids about what they think are the very best things in life. Ask them to do or answer the following: "Describe your best vacation." "Tell about your happiest moment." "What was your best meal ever?" "What's the most beautiful thing you ever saw?" "Tell us about a time when you felt incredible peace." "When did you feel the proudest?" "What did it feel like to win a championship or accomplish something special?" As your kids describe these things they will be identifying times of joy, contentment, peace, beauty, meaning, and goodness.

Then ask, "Where did all these good things come from?" Have your child read James 1:17, which tells us that everything good and perfect comes from God. Then tell them that all the good things and perfect things that come from God come out of his holiness, his pure goodness. The very nature of our great God is holy and perfect and good!

Tell your kids repeatedly that because God's nature is holy he will never ask them to do anything that would not be right and good for them. It is out of this pure goodness that he wants to protect them from those things that would harm them and provide for their very best. It is from his holy nature of goodness that he gives unselfishly and makes the security, happiness, and welfare of your kids as important as his own. They need to know that he, by his very nature, is *that good.* Tell them you are in awe of his holiness and goodness. He is an awesome God.

God is a great God. He is pure goodness through and through. He is a God to be in awe of. But there is more. His holiness may make him pure goodness, but it is his relational heart that makes him infinitely loving.

Living in Awe of God's Relational Heart

When the almighty God spoke the words, "Let there be...," the world was created (Genesis 1:3). Because he is pure goodness by nature, what he created was good. After each creation day, "God saw that it was good" (Genesis 1:10). But he didn't create as a unitary—singular—being. He didn't create alone. God created as a triune relationship, because all three persons of the Godhead were there at creation.

"The Spirit of God was hovering over the surface of the waters" (Genesis 1:2). God the Son, who was born on earth as Jesus, was there too. "Christ is the visible image of the invisible God. He existed before anything was created and is supreme over all creation, for through him God created everything" (Colossians 1:15-16). This triune aspect of God demonstrates that he is a relational being. Before there were humans, before Planet Earth or the universe or time as we know it, he existed eternally as Relationship.

God did not create humans because he needed relationships—he already existed as relationship. He created us as his children to lovingly relate to him as our Father. As we mentioned earlier, God is not an autocratic rule-enforcing Father, nor is he a permissive or an inattentive Father. Rather, he is the ultimate as a relationally loving God, and he wants us to enjoy the goodness of life in relationship with him.

King David described God's relational heart this way:

> The Lord is compassionate and merciful, slow to get angry and filled with unfailing love (Psalm 103:8).
>
> Your faithfulness extends to every generation...Lord, how great is your mercy (Psalm 119:90,156).
>
> He gives justice to the oppressed and food to the hungry. The Lord frees the prisoners. The Lord opens the eyes of the blind. The Lord lifts up those who are weighed down. The Lord loves the godly. The Lord protects the foreigners among us. He cares for the orphans and widows, but he frustrates the plans of the wicked (Psalm 146:7-9).
>
> He heals the brokenhearted and bandages their wounds (Psalm 147:3).

God is compassionate, merciful, unfailing, faithful, just, and caring. His pure heart protects the ones he loves and provides for their good. His love is giving and trusting, unselfish and sacrificial, secure and safe, loyal and forever.

When you love your children as God does, you make their security, happiness, and welfare as important as your own. And when you do, you reveal to your kids the very heart of God. Scripture says that when we love as he loves we become "mirrors that brightly reflect the glory of the Lord. And as the Spirit of the Lord works within us, we become more and more like him and reflect his glory even more" (2 Corinthians 3:18 NLT).

Do you get the picture? You are to be a loving dad who places all the rules and instruction you give to your children within the context of a loving relationship. Why? Because all those instructions and guidelines are designed to provide for your children's good and protect them from harm. This reflects God's heart. That is the way he treats us. When you raise your children "with the discipline and instruction that come from the Lord" (Ephesians 6:4), you are acting like God and you become a mirror of his relational heart. That is how you are to introduce him to your kids—as the "God who is passionate about his relationship with [them]" (Exodus 34:14 NLT).

Tell each of your children often "to fear [be in awe of] the Lord your God, to walk in all his ways and love Him, and to serve the Lord your God with all your heart and with all your soul, and to keep the Lord's commandments and His statutes *which I am commanding you today for your good*" (Deuteronomy 10:12-13 NASB). Let your kids know that everything God does comes from his holy nature of goodness expressed through his relational heart of love. Repeat that theme to them over and over again. He does what he does because he loves us, and it is always for our best!

A Unique Way to Reveal God's Heart to Your Kids

It is impossible to grasp or express God's infinite characteristics. We cannot fathom his holy nature of goodness. Yet he created us as relational beings to relate to his relational heart. While we by no means can comprehend his heart exhaustively, we are powerfully drawn to him and can relate to him truly. We were created to love him back and love others as we love ourselves.

The tragedy is that the first human couple chose to doubt the goodness and relational heart of God. When they were tempted, they chose to doubt that he had their best interest at heart when he commanded them not to eat the fruit of the tree in the middle of the Garden of Eden. The rejection of his relationship with them, which he had created good and perfect, was an affront to him. Humans rebelled against him. They sinned and "it broke his heart" (Genesis 6:6).

Remember that God by his very nature is holy. He cannot be in relationship with sin in any manner. Scripture says, "Your eyes are too pure to look on evil; you cannot tolerate wrongdoing" (Habakkuk 1:13 NIV). As another translation puts it, he is so holy that he "cannot allow sin in any form" (Habakkuk 1:13 NLT). To do so would violate the very essence of who he is. His only choice was to separate himself from sinful humans, which brought spiritual and physical death upon them.

But instead of leaving humans eternally alone, separated from him in their sin, he reached out in love to draw them back to him.

> God is so rich in mercy, and he loved us so much, that even though we were dead because of our sins, he gave us life when he raised Christ from the dead (Ephesians 2:4-5).

The cost, of course, was the torturous death of his Son on a cruel cross. The innocent and holy Son was willing to suffer and die so he could restore a relationship with you and me. God's pure goodness would not allow him to be with us, but his relational heart could not stand to be without us. When that reality dawns on our hearts it causes us to be in awe of his mercy, love, and grace.

How do we convey that awesome truth to our kids? If they could somehow catch a glimpse of God's relational heart they would be powerfully drawn to him.

For years I have attempted to help dads and moms lead their kids to Christ. My entire life has been about evangelism largely to youth. And I made leading my own kids to Christ a priority in my life. But how do you actually lead a child to the point of a miraculous, transformed relationship with God?

Often our kids come to trust in Christ personally through a church service, youth-group meeting, youth camp, or a large youth event. Other times a parent actually prays with his or her child to accept Christ. A few years back we devised a tool a parent could use in a family setting to reveal God's true heart. This tool is in a story form—countless families have used it individually or in a group setting. Often three or four families get together for what we call a "Redemption Celebration." This celebration is drawn from the Old Testament Passover meal and made applicable to Christ as the sacrificial lamb. I have provided on my website the entire "Redemption

Celebration" event with all the instructions for you to conduct it yourself. *

Leading your child to trust in Jesus as their Savior is one of the most thrilling experiences you can have as a dad. But remember, it is ultimately each child's own choice whether he or she trusts in Christ or not. You are only responsible to lead them to God by making a commitment to do your best to explain who he is and what he is like.

---

* For a free download, simply go to www.josh.org/RC1 and follow the links to all the instructions and presentations you need in order to conduct your own Redemption Celebration.

7

COMMITMENT #5

I Will Do My Best to
Instill a Love of Self That Is Unselfish

Dad, make Megan give me back my Game Boy."

"Megan, give Ari his Game Boy."

"Dad, he's had it all day. It's my turn."

"Ari, it's Megan's turn."

"That's not fair, Dad. It's my Game Boy!"

"Megan, it's his Game Boy."

"Here take your *@x# Game Boy!"

"Megan Kathleen, we don't use that kind of language in this family!"

Sound familiar? Our kids are not naturally giving and unselfish. They may be reluctant to share. They might even throw a Game Boy, iPhone, or e-reader in disgust at a sibling. So trying to instill a love of self may seem like fueling the problem. The truth is, however, the basis of an unselfish and other-focused love is a healthy love of self.

It Is Not Selfish to Love Yourself

It was one of those days. You're heading home from work and you're tired and hungry. As you walk through the door the aroma of your favorite meal greets you. Your spouse has gotten off early from work and decided to fix you a meal fit for a king.

You savor each bite, and when your plate is nearly empty you reach for a second helping. Question: Are you being selfish to satisfy your hunger?

After the meal you take a long hot shower, slip into some comfortable clothes, and lie down on the couch. Question: Are you being selfish to relax after a long day?

The next morning after a good night's sleep you head out for an invigorating jog. An oncoming car swerves to miss an animal and comes a little too close for comfort. You jump to the curb for safety. Question: Are you being selfish to avoid being hit by a car?

All the time, you feed yourself, find ways to relax, try to get enough sleep, and protect your body. Are you being selfish in doing so? Or are you simply loving yourself to take proper care of yourself?

The apostle Paul told us husbands to love our wives as we love our own bodies. "Husbands ought to love their wives as they love their own bodies. For a man who loves his wife shows love for himself. No one hates his own body but feeds and cares for it, just as Christ cares for the church" (Ephesians 5:28-29). What this passage assumes is that we care enough about ourselves to properly provide for what we need and protect ourselves from harm. It is appropriate and healthy to look out for our own security, happiness, and welfare. We are not being selfish when we do this—we are simply respecting and valuing ourselves as a person created in the image of God with infinite dignity and worth. In fact, Paul is implying here that we can't properly love our wives unless we properly love ourselves.

Jesus said that each of us is to love God with our everything and then "love your neighbor as yourself" (Matthew 22:39). Here it is again—love of self is a prerequisite to loving others. Jesus certainly isn't advocating a narcissism that focuses on a selfish pursuit in life. Rather he is acknowledging our intrinsic value and worth as God's creation and that it's natural and proper to provide for and protect what he has made. And so we ought to love others in the same way we want to be loved. That is why Jesus said, "Do to others whatever you would like them to do to you. This is the essence of all that is taught in the law and the prophets" (Matthew 7:12). I simply contend we can't love others as God commands until and unless we have a healthy love of ourselves. In other words, we are to have a healthy sense of self-worth. If we don't properly value and love ourselves, we are going to have a tough time knowing how to love others as we should.

Now I admit that some people doubt it's biblical to focus on such things as self-love or self-worth. After speaking, I am often challenged by some who are disturbed that I talk about a worth of self. They contend that the concept of self-worth focuses attention on self instead of God.

Whenever I am challenged this way, I usually respond by saying something like this: "I agree that we can become self-centered and all wrapped up in our own self-interests, but I don't agree that self-worth is a sinful idea. In fact, I believe that a proper understanding of our worth and value as God's creation is exactly what keeps us from becoming selfish and self-centered. The apostle Paul encouraged 'everyone among you not to think more highly of himself than he ought to think; but to think so as to have sound judgment, as God has allotted to each a measure of faith' (Romans 12:3 NASB)."

Paul is not saying in this verse that we should not think highly of ourselves. He says that we should not think more highly of ourselves than *what we really are*. In other words, we should be realistic and biblical in our opinions of ourselves. That's why Paul added that we are "to think so as to have sound judgment."

The verb *to think* in the Greek means "to think or to feel in a certain way [about a person]." In Romans 12:3, it refers to "forming an opinion, a judgment, or a feeling about yourself."[1] Paul's point is that we should form this opinion or self-concept as a result of a realistic appraisal of ourselves based on God's view of us. It is not being selfish to accept his view of ourselves; it is being biblical.

Being selfish is looking out for number one regardless of how it affects others. Having a healthy self-worth is foundational in resisting a selfish attitude. When Jesus told us to love others as we love ourselves he was saying we should love others in the same way we want to be loved—in the same way we want to be provided for and protected.

As we pointed out in a previous chapter, loving others as we love ourselves actually defines a Godlike love. It is a love that not only looks out for "your own interests, but...to the interest of others" (Philippians 2:4 NIV). A love based on a healthy self-worth makes the security, happiness, and welfare of another person as important as your own.

When you instill a love of self that is unselfish within your kids, you are actually cultivating a healthy sense of self-worth in them. As you do you are helping them realize who they are—a person with value and dignity who is loved for who they are. We talked before about the need for your kids to feel accepted unconditionally and how that gives them a sense of security. When your kids realize that your acceptance of them is based on their self-worth as your son or daughter, they gain a sense of identity. When each of your kids feel valued as your son or daughter, they are able to love themselves unselfishly. They then have the biblical emotional basis to love others as they love themselves.

How to Cultivate a Healthy Self-Worth in Your Kids

I have gotten a lot of e-mails and letters over the years from teenagers struggling with their sense of worth. One girl wrote me and said, "Josh, I know at least twenty people I'd rather be than myself." She obviously had a poor sense of her own self-worth. A young man wrote, "I'm alone and confused. I just don't feel that my life is worth living anymore. I cry myself to sleep every night. Sometimes I just wish I were dead." These kids, like so many, don't feel a sense of intrinsic value. And many times it is because they have bought into certain myths propagated by the culture around them. You can begin to cultivate a sense of self-worth in your kids by actively countering the following three myths.

Myth #1: Image Is Everything

A pleasant and attractive physical appearance is one of the most highly valued personal attributes in our culture today. And your kids know it. They are constantly asking themselves, *How do I look?* Kids tend to formulate their sense of self-worth from the praise or criticism they receive from other people based on their appearance.

It all begins in childhood. Sadly, kids can be mercilessly unkind in the way they talk about how people look. Has your child ever been called names like Four Eyes, Big Nose, or Lard Bottom by his or her peers? If so, his or her sense of worth was probably negatively affected. Physical appearance and the image that creates will seem like everything to your kids at some point in their life. Here are some steps you can take to counter that myth.

Let each of your kids know they are unique individuals who stand out as beautiful and valuable in their uniqueness. Think of it: Of the more than 7 billion people alive right now on Planet Earth, there is no one just like your child. No one has the exact appearance you do and your child does. None of us can take credit or blame for how we look and how we're constructed. Encourage your kids to accept and appreciate the way God has made them and accept their body and appearance as his gift to them. We shouldn't be proud of something we had nothing to do with—and none of us had anything to do with how we look.

However, we can take a healthy pride in what we do with our appearance. You can encourage your kids to enhance their appearance in numerous ways, but be sure they grasp the amazing truth that they are unique. Capitalize on that uniqueness and let each of your children know they are special, one-of-a-kind originals. This will help them realize their value and worth to God.

Have you ever stepped outside on a winter's morning as the soft flakes of snow drifted slowly to the ground? If you could inspect the microscopic details of the tiny snowflakes landing on your sleeve you would see, of course, that each has a distinct shape. You've probably seen a photograph or video that magnifies a snowflake—if so, you've certainly marveled at the intricate shape, structure, and beauty of that single flake. And undoubtedly you've heard scientists claim that no two snowflakes are alike. They are all one-of-a-kind originals.

You and I and your kids are each one-of-a-kind originals designed uniquely by God. Each of us has been given a distinct and special identity that makes us unique. God has placed deep within your kids special gifts, talents, and passions, as well as distinct personalities, that make them uniquely special. If you have two children, you can probably see a likeness between them that comes from being of the same family. Yet you also know that each child is different because no two children are alike. Each of them has a quality and distinct value that makes them an original—one-of-a-kind.

One of the indications that Scripture recognizes a child's unique-ness is found in the familiar words penned by King Solomon: "Train up a child in the way he should go, even when he is old he will not depart from it" (Proverbs 22:6 NASB).

Unfortunately, this verse is often misunderstood and misapplied. Many dads think it means, "Have family devotions, make sure kids attend church and youth group and a Christian school, and when they are grown up, they will not depart from the faith."

The real emphasis of this verse, however, centers on the phrase "the way he [or she] should go." The writer is referring to the *child's* way, his or her leaning or bent. The root meanings of these words suggest stimulating a desire for guidance according to each child's own uniqueness.

The same Hebrew word that is used in Proverbs 22 is translated "bend" in two psalms and refers to the bending of an archer's bow (see Psalm 11:2; 64:3). Today, with precision manufacturing, almost any-one can pick up a bow with a 45-pound draw weight and do a fair job of hitting a target. But in biblical days, nothing was standardized. All archers made their own bows and had to know the unique char-acteristics of that bow if they hoped to hit anything with it.

God's Word is telling us that your child has an inborn uniqueness that you need to identify and train accordingly. In the *Ryrie Study Bible*, a note for Proverbs 22:6 explains that

> "the way he should go" really means "according to his way; i.e., the child's habits and interests." The instruction must take into account his individuality and inclinations, his personality, the unique way God created him, and must be in keeping with his physical and mental development. [2]

The apostle Paul explains that "God has given each of us the ability to do certain things well" (Romans 12:6). He goes on to enumerate those things and admonish us regarding the attitude and relationships in which we are to exercise the gifts and abilities God has given each of us. It is clear we all have been given gifts that are distinct to us. It is this distinctiveness that further underscores our unique self-worth.

Your kids may intuitively realize they are originals. But make sure they understand their uniqueness. Their personal identification is distinctly them. Their fingerprints are unique; their retina scans are distinct; their faces and bodies are all slightly different. Help them understand that their uniqueness makes them of great value:

- God has chosen *special gifts* just for them by which they can express their love and care for others. He has placed deep within your kids a natural bent that makes up the constellation of their gifts and unique interests. They are to use them within his and your family as only they can. Help them identify those gifts and celebrate their worth with them.

- God has also given your kids built-in preferences: things like how they are energized, how they process information, and how they make decisions. These things make up their *distinct personality*. Guide your children to know their distinct personalities and then celebrate their worth with them.

- God has instilled in your kids certain *passions*: things they feel strongly about, things they're fervently interested in, and things that give them a special sense of joy when they talk about them or pursue them. Those passions direct them to who, where, and what he wants them to love in life…as only they can. Work to identify their God-given passions in life and then celebrate their worth with them.

God has uniquely shaped and molded you and your kids to bring honor to him. It is only proper and right to love what he has done. Teaching your kids to love what he has uniquely designed isn't being self-centered. We need to be proud of him for what he has created and humbly celebrate our uniqueness for his glory, "for everything comes from him and exists by his power and is intended for his glory. All glory to him forever! Amen" (Romans 11:36).

When you were growing up, your parents may have understood that you were a one-of-a-kind individual and sought to train you up in "the way you should go." If so, you have no doubt come a long way in identifying your personality type, special gifts, and passions in life. But if you are like most of us, you have only a partial understanding of your identity and consequently your sense of self-worth. And if so, you may struggle to help your children unlock the secret to their identities and self-worth too. That is why most of us dads could use some help in guiding our kids to realize their uniqueness and sense of worth.

Perhaps no other book and course can better help you accomplish that than the book and workbook *Find Your Fit* by Jane Kise and

Kevin Johnson. I have drawn much of what I have said here about what makes each of us unique from their book and workbook.*

You can actually walk your own kids through the *Find Your Fit* material as a family experience. Discover your true value as God's unique individuals together as a family. And as you do you will be shattering the myth that image is everything.

Myth #2: You Are What You Do

Let's face it—we live in a performance-based culture. The task-oriented society your kids are growing up in values them largely based on how much they do and how well they do it. Of course you want your children to make good grades, excel in sports, and do well in band, ballet, dance, and so on. What you want to avoid is for them to feel that their performance defines their self-worth.

It was time for the big season to start. My son, Sean, was 12 at the time and ready to play Little League baseball. Before the first game I got an idea about how to teach him—and his teammates—an important lesson about his value as a person rather than just a player. I bought 12 coupons good for ice-cream sundaes at a local restaurant and took them to the baseball coach.

"Coach, these are for the kids," I said.

"Good," the coach said with a big smile. "This is great. I wish more dads took an interest like this. I'll take them for sundaes after our first win."

"No, Coach," I said quickly. "I want you to take them for sundaes after their first *loss*."

The coach looked at me strangely. What I was saying wasn't computing with his concept of winning, losing, and rewards for good play. So I proceeded to explain my thinking.

---

* Kevin has devoted his life to ministering to young people and helping parents successfully guide their young people through a godless culture. Jane has an extensive background in career counseling of both young people and adults. To check out what they have available go to www.LifeKeys .com. You will also find there is a book and course for adults on their site called *Discover Who You Are*. Check it out.

"Coach, I don't know about you, but as I raise my kids I don't want to acknowledge their success as much as their effort. And I don't want to acknowledge their effort as much as their being someone who was created in the image of God. I believe my son is created in God's image and that he has infinite value, dignity, and worth. None of these things have anything to do with playing baseball. If he never played baseball an inning in his life, I would love and accept him as a person of great worth."

The coach looked at me for a long moment. Finally, all he could muster was, "That's weird!" But he agreed to use the coupons as I instructed.

The season started and Sean's team won their first few games. But they lost the third or fourth game, and the coach was true to his word. He gave each player an ice-cream sundae coupon and they all went out to "celebrate" their loss.

Sean must have thanked me at least five times for the sundaes. And over the next two weeks three of the kids on his team came up and thanked me too. One of his teammates, a boy named Jesse, came up to me and said, "Thanks a lot for the ice-cream sundaes, Mr. McDowell. Wow! It doesn't matter to you if we win or not—you think we're great anyway."

What I wanted to communicate to Sean and his teammates was that their worth wasn't based on their ability to win baseball games. It was based upon the fact they had dignity, value, and worth by virtue of being created in God's image. And additionally, Sean's worth to me was based on the fact that he was my son and I was his dad.

Take every opportunity to let your kids know they are of great value to you because of who they are—your son or your daughter. It's not that their accomplishments shouldn't be recognized. They should be. But your kids need to understand that their accomplishments or failures don't define their worth.

An excellent time to shatter the "you are what you do" myth is when your kids get their report cards. When your child gets good grades, say something like, "I so appreciate the hard work you're put-ting in to make those A's. But you know, I don't love and respect you because you're a good student. If you never got an A, I'd love you just as much."

Focus more on your kids' worth as a person than on their perfor-mance by using phrases such as

- "You're really creative."
- "You've got a great sense of humor."
- "I love your enthusiasm."
- "You have such a caring heart."

When we focus on such qualities as diligence, dependability, cre-ativity, courage, persistence, and patience in our kids, we communi-cate that they are of worth based on who they are, not just for what they do. As you do this your son or your daughter will gain a greater sense of self-worth. They will learn to love themselves for who they are, and that will give them the healthy basis to love others.

Myth #3: You Are Somebody Only If You Have Status

This myth surfaces when we answer the question *How important am I?* If your child associates importance with such things as being popular, hanging with the "in crowd," having all the designer clothes, or being voted class president, then they've probably bought into the status myth propagated by our culture. Most kids, and many adults, don't feel good about themselves unless they have significant power, influence, or control over others. Their identity and sense of worth is wrapped up in the amount of status they can achieve in the eyes of the world. I call this "cultural status." And when this kind of sta-tus is lost, their self-worth drops to the basement.

The reason cultural status doesn't define us as being somebody is because that type of status is the wrong measurement for our self-concept. The cultural status that most kids (and adults) chase after is empty, fleeting, and exhausting. They may be popular today because they're the homecoming queen or the basketball star. But that is short-lived. That's what makes achieving cultural status so exhausting—it is a constant chase to try to maintain it. King Solomon spoke of the futility of trying to maintain this kind of status.

> A youth could rise from poverty and succeed. He might even become king…But then everyone rushes to the side of yet another youth who replaces him. Endless crowds stand around him, but then another generation grows up and rejects him too. So it is all meaningless— like chasing the wind (Ecclesiastes 4:14-16).

Your child's worth is not meant to be determined by their physical appearance, what they do, or any cultural status they chase after. Their worth has already been established by God, who created them in his image. Your task is to reinforce and solidify that worth so each of them will accept and own it personally.

It has been said that our self-concept is determined largely by what we believe the most important person in our lives thinks about us. If my wife, for example, tells me I'm a considerate husband, I'll tend to believe her, because she is the most important woman in my life. And if she thinks that about me, I'll consider it true about me.

God has already stated our worth, and if he is the most important person in our lives then we need to accept his valuation of us as our self-concept. Jesus said some very significant things about those who have accepted him: "I have loved you," he said, "even as the Father has loved me…I have told you these things so that you will be filled with my joy…I no longer call you slaves, because a master doesn't confide in his slaves. Now you are my friends, since I have told you everything the Father told me. You didn't choose me, I chose you" (John 15:9,11,15-16).

According to Jesus Christ you are loved, his friend, and chosen by him! The apostle Paul goes on to add to the list. Remember the following things are *already* true of you. You didn't earn these things or attain them because of some status you may have achieved. This is what God's Word says about you.

- You are "blessed…with every spiritual blessing" (Ephesians 1:3).

- "God chose [you] in Christ to be holy and without fault in his eyes" (verse 4).

- "God decided in advance to adopt [you] into his family" (verse 5).

- "He purchased [your] freedom with the blood of his Son and forgave [your] sins" (verse 7).

- You "have received an inheritance from God" (verse 11).

- He has "seated [you] with him in the heavenly realms" (Ephesians 2:6).

- You "are God's masterpiece" (verse 10).

- "You belong to Christ" (verse 13 NLT).

- "Nothing can ever separate [you] from God's love" (Romans 8:38).

As his child these are just some of the things God thinks and says about you. Since your heavenly Father is the most important person in your life, believe these things, accept them, and own them as your own. Allow what he thinks and says to reinforce your worth to him. As you do you will enjoy a healthy sense of self-worth.

You can reinforce the worth of your kids in a similar manner. Use the cultural-status myth your kids may tend to adopt to your advantage. But switch the focus away from the cultural symbols to you—you're the one who owns the status of being their father. Do the same with God, who owns the status of being their heavenly Father. Say these kinds of things often to your kids:

- "I am proud to be called your dad."

- "God is proud to be called your heavenly Father too."
- "God meant you to be part of this family and I'm so glad he did."
- "God also adopted you into his family."
- "There is nothing you could ever do against me that would keep me from forgiving you."
- "God's forgiveness is always there for you too."
- "There is no one in the world like you—I'm so proud you're my son/daughter."
- "You are God's unique masterpiece."
- "You bear my last name—you belong to this family."
- "You belong to Jesus and his family too."
- "There is nothing you could ever do that would sever the tie of my love for you—you will always be my son, my daughter, who I love."
- "Nothing can ever separate you from God's love either."

Your kids may not always know or feel their true sense of worth, but you do. Take every opportunity to break through the exterior and masks your kids learn to put on and let them know how valuable they are to you. If you would like more help on building up your own sense of self-worth I recommend a book I wrote awhile back entitled *See Yourself as God Sees You.* Check it out at www.josh.org.

As you let your kids know how much you, their father, and God, their heavenly Father, value them they will slowly but surely gain a healthy sense of self-worth. You will then be instilling in them a love of self that is unselfish.

8

I Will Do My Best to Impart God's Way of Forming Healthy Love Relationships

The wedding music begins to play as you and your family are seated. A relative is getting married and your wife, son, and daughter are there with you to witness the ceremony.

Your daughter leans toward you and begins to talk softly. "Dad, will the vows cousin Sara makes today really stick? I mean, isn't that what true love is supposed to do—make a marriage last forever?"

Before you can answer your son overhears and interrupts. "You can't love someone forever, dumbhead. I mean nobody loves forever—right, Dad?"

"Nobody's talking to you, lizard breath," your daughter fires back. "What I mean, Dad, is when I find that special man in my life I want it to be true love. So how do I make sure it's true love—a love that will last forever?"

"Tell her, Dad," your son interjects. "Tell her no one is going to love her for five minutes, let alone forever."

Now it's not likely that your kids are going to put those questions to you quite like that. But you can be sure that, at some point, they will want to know what makes for a true love relationship. As they begin to enter adulthood their interest in love and relationships increases. I remember at one point my daughters seemed to go through boyfriends on almost a weekly basis. And that was a prime time to help them, and my son, to understand what real love does and what real love is.

In a previous chapter we defined real love as making the security, happiness, and welfare of another person as important as your own. When a love relationship is rooted in the concept of making the interests of another as important as your own (love your neighbor as yourself), it becomes a healthy one.

However, what our kids hear and see in today's culture is rarely a representation of a healthy love. Selfish, lustful, and even abusive behavior is often passed off as a love relationship. That is why, in a real sense, we must redefine to our kids what such a relationship actually is from a biblical perspective. By the time a typical child reaches ten years old he or she probably has a distorted concept of how a person in a loving relationship acts. And as dads, along with our wives, we need to correct these distortions by reintroducing our kids to what makes a love relationship healthy. Over time I discovered at least five biblical components that make such relationships healthy. Imparting these truths on them to your kids will go a long way in helping them form healthy relationships with others.

A Healthy Love Relationship Is God's Idea

Forming a healthy love relationship with another person wasn't a human idea. Humans didn't create love, God did. When Scripture says, "God is love" (1 John 4:16) it means more than God loves us. He is the very meaning and essence of what a love relationship is all about.

God, consisting as he does of three persons—Father, Son, and Holy Spirit—demonstrates that loving relationships have existed eternally. God exists in relationship. The Father has always infinitely loved the Son. The Son has always and eternally loved the Father. The Holy Spirit has forever loved both the Father and the Son. The absolute standard of a healthy love relationship has been established by God. This continuous cycle of a perfect relationship is ever being experienced within the Godhead. It is our model of what a healthy relationship is all about.

Created in God's image, we were meant to love both him and others as he loves. He loves perfectly and he wants to teach us how to love in a healthy way. Jesus said, "Just as I have loved you, you should love each other" (John 13:34). Jesus is the model of healthy, loving relationships. His kind of love bonds us together, gives joy and meaning to life, and does in fact last. That is what our kids and all of us seek—loving relationships that complete us, give us inner peace, and make life worth living. We all want a perfect love like that, and it all originates in and from God. He "is love, and all who live in love live in God, and God lives in them. And as we live in God, our love grows more perfect" (1 John 4:16-17).

A Healthy Love Relationship Is Other-Focused

"This is real love," Scripture states, "not that we loved God, but that he loved us and sent his Son as a sacrifice to take away our sins" (1 John 4:10). If a healthy love relationship is anything, it is other-focused. Jesus wasn't looking out for his personal interest when he entered our world to die for us. He was focused on us and what we needed. That is what true love does.

What holds a true love relationship together is the deep desire of two people, each looking out for the best interest of the other. Love is not self-centered; "it does not demand its own way" (1 Corinthians 13:5). In a healthy love relationship each person is looking to provide for the other's best and protect the other from the worst.

The concept of this "other focus" kind of love relationship isn't necessarily easy to convey to your kids. You don't have to be very observant to recognize that your kids are self-centered by nature.

Did you ever have your child grab a toy out of your hand and authoritatively announce, "Mine"? We all have something within us that fears we won't get what is due us or that somehow we won't get to enjoy what truly belongs to us. So we naturally tend to take rather than freely give. Sharing "toys" with others or giving of our time to others, let alone sacrificing for someone else, doesn't at first seem to be in our best interest. But the reality is, God made giving to others the cornerstone of healthy relationships. Actually, giving to others *is* in our best interest.

Jesus said, "Give, and you will receive. Your gift will return to you in full…The amount you give will determine the amount you get back" (Luke 6:38). This is one of the reciprocal principles of a healthy loving relationship. We get what we give. To give out and to think of the interest of others first doesn't leave us without and wanting—it actually is what gives us fulfillment.

I remember a time Sean and I were in a downtown area of San Diego. We had stopped at a fast-food restaurant to get a bite to eat. We ordered one large sandwich and were going to share it with each other.

We found a bench outside and started to split the sandwich, when we saw what appeared to be a homeless man sitting on a bench next to us. I looked at Sean and motioned toward the man. "I bet he's hungry too," I whispered. "Want to share our sandwich with him?" I asked.

"I'm really hungry, Dad," my son responded. "I'm hungry too," I replied. "But I bet he's a lot hungrier than we are. Trust me, we'll have enough to eat even if we share our food." Somewhat reluctantly Sean nodded in approval.

I told the gentleman, whose name was Allen, that my son and I had a large sandwich and we'd be glad to share it if he was hungry. He smiled, joined us on our bench, and we each enjoyed a third of a sandwich.

As we chatted we learned that Allen was in fact homeless. He had a rather sad story to share and we both listened intently. I related a little of my own story, including how I became a Christian. Before it was all over Sean and I prayed with Allen and he left feeling as though someone cared about him.

As Sean and I drove back up to our mountain home from San Diego he said, "Dad, I only had a third of a sandwich but I feel like I've eaten two sandwiches. It's so great that we gave part of our meal to Allen. I think we really encouraged him." I took the opportunity to explain that when we give to others and trust God for our needs, he'll always take care of us. He sees to it that we get back what we give, either in this life or the next.

Challenge your kids to give of their time and what they have to others. Even young children can be taught the many rewards of giving. It can be extremely fulfilling to a child to give a portion of their allowance to needy children in a foreign country. Many relief organizations are structured to encourage children to give to children; they provide ways to exchange pictures and letters. Involving your children in efforts that are other-focused like that teaches them the nature of God's kind of love.

Modeling this kind of other-focused attitude and action before your kids is also essential. Be transparent about past and current relationships in which you made sacrifices of your time, energy, and possessions. Let them know how much you received in return. Sharing your own experiences will reinforce that giving and being other-focused keeps relationships strong and is incredibly rewarding and fulfilling.

A Healthy Love Relationship Must Receive in Order to Give

A fact of life is that we can't give what we don't have. And that extends to loving relationships. We actually give of ourselves to others based on what we have received. The apostle John wrote, "This is real love—not that we loved God, but that he loved us...We love each other because he loved us first" (1 John 4:10,19).

The power to form healthy, loving relationships with others comes from accepting a healthy, loving relationship from God and others. God doesn't ask us to forgive others, accept without condition, enter a person's world to show attention, or demonstrate affection, appreciation, and so on, without first loving us in that way. For example, the apostle Paul said, "Accept each other just as Christ has accepted you" (Romans 15:7). Receiving Christ's acceptance empowers us to accept others. We are able to give of ourselves and form healthy love relationships because God and others have relationally given so much to us.

Think of people you know who struggle forming healthy love relationships. Most likely they have experienced broken and dysfunctional relationships in their past. If we have experienced healthy relationships in our past, they will foster present and future ones. But if we have experienced past dysfunctional relationships it will foster present and future dysfunctional relationships. Somewhere along the line the cycle of dysfunction must be broken, and that begins by getting in a position to receive healthy Godlike relationships.

As I've said, I grew up in a seriously dysfunctional home. I really didn't know how to give or receive love. And I was destined to pass on that dysfunctional pattern within my future marriage and family unless and until I was able to lock into a new and healthy way of relating to God, myself, and others.

As I went through high school and on to college, I was hungry to experience a family where real, loving relationships were present. I was fortunate to find a godly family like that—the Dick and Charlotte Day family.

I met Dick when we were both in seminary during the 1960s. Dick was a few years older than the rest of us, married and with four children. He had come to Christ in his late twenties and felt called to the ministry. We met while registering for seminary classes and hit it off immediately.

I soon became virtually another member of the Day family, often stopping by at interesting hours such as 6:30 a.m. or after 11:00 p.m. to talk about something I felt couldn't wait. Dick was always patient, kind, loving—all traits that I had known very little of while growing up.

I was impressed immediately by how Dick and Charlotte treated their children and each other. They accepted and appreciated their kids, always encouraging them and making them feel worthwhile and important. And they loved them with affectionate words and touching—lots of hugging. You might say I learned to hug by hanging around the Day family. And they were always available. They always had time for their kids, something that impressed me because my father never seemed to have time for me.

Another thing I noticed was that the Days thanked their kids for what they did around the house. Taking out the garbage, cleaning up—whatever it was—they always made it a point to show their children appreciation for what they did. As I looked back on my own childhood, I remembered that my father had taught me how to work. I could give him that much. But his appreciation of what I did? I couldn't remember much, if any, of that.

In a real sense, Dick's family became the family I never had. I learned the meaning of healthy relationships from receiving their love and giving that kind of love in return. If you struggle from a dysfunctional past (and all of us do to some degree or another), find a mature couple who knows the meaning of a biblical, healthy relationship and hang around them. Ask the mature dad—maybe he's even a grandfather—to be your mentor. You will not only honor him with your request, but he can also give to you relationally so you can more effectively give to your kids.

A Healthy Love Relationship Meets the Needs of Others

The expression used most often to describe Jesus' heart of love was that he was "moved with compassion." When he saw the two blind men he was "moved with compassion." When he saw the leper he was "moved with compassion." When he saw the sick and the hungry he was "moved with compassion."* Jesus' heart of love moved him to put others first, largely by meeting people at the point of their need

---

* See Matthew 9:36; 14:14; 15:32; 20:34; Mark 1:41; 6:34; 8:2.

of the moment, whether that was a physical, relational, or spiritual need. That is what we do in loving relationships—we meet others at the point of their need of the moment.

When your first child came into the world, one of the first things you probably noticed was his or her ability to get attention. Newborn babies have strong vocal cords and yours probably made good use of them. And one of the reasons your child made his or her voice heard was to let you know "I'm hungry." I'm sure you and your wife met your child's need of the moment and fed him or her. When your child digested the milk or formula you met his or her need of the moment and changed the diaper. When he or she got sleepy you met the need of the moment and provided a safe and comfortable place to sleep. Providing for your children's physical needs has been something you have done from day one. That's part of what loving your kids looks like.

Loving our kids also involves meeting the needs of the moment for them relationally. Just like there are physical needs, there are also relational needs. As we meet the relational needs of our kids it actually empowers them to in turn learn how to meet the relational needs of the moment for others. That's part of what healthy relationships do.

That's what I observed in the Day family. They were other-focused on meeting each other's relational needs of the moment. Dick and Charlotte gave need-meeting love to their kids, and as each child had their relational needs met for acceptance, appreciation, affection, and so on, it empowered them to do the same for others.

For years I wasn't sure I knew all the relational needs my kids had. I wasn't even certain I knew what all mine were or those of Dottie. We have already mentioned a number of them in previous chapters— for example, the needs to be accepted, appreciated, affirmed, shown attention, and made accountable. Scripture identifies at least 35 of these relational needs that we have on one level or another. We refer to them as the "one anothers" of Scripture, for example, "accept one another" (Romans 15:7), "care for [give attention to] one another" (1 Corinthians 12:25), "encourage one another" (1 Thessalonians 5:11), and so on. A dear friend of mine, Dr. David Ferguson, introduced me to these Scripture passages and explained how to identify the top ten relational needs in a person's life in order of their priority. This has proven invaluable in helping me take specific steps to meet the relational needs of the moment of both my wife and my kids.

Of course you can find these relational needs all throughout Scripture. But let's identify just ten of them, define them, and give a Scripture reference for each. As you read through these, try to identify which ones are the highest priorities for each of your children. I will define these needs in the first person by how your child might feel when you take steps to meet them.

- *The relational need for acceptance.* I feel accepted when you love me without condition, especially when my behavior has been less than perfect; it is making me feel loved for who I really am (Romans 15:7).

- *The relational need for attention (care).* I feel cared for when you enter my world and demonstrate your interest and concern for me (1 Corinthians 12:25).

- *The relational need for approval.* I feel approved of when you express satisfaction with me as a person and demonstrate you are pleased with me (Romans 14:18).

- *The relational need for appreciation.* I feel appreciated when you praise me and communicate gratefulness for one of my accomplishments or efforts (1 Corinthians 11:2).

- *The relational need for comfort (affirmation).* I feel comforted when you grieve with me when I hurt and you identify with a measure of the pain I feel (2 Corinthians 1:3-4).

- *The relational need for support.* I feel support when you come alongside me to help lift my load and help me carry a struggle or problem (Galatians 6:2).

- *The relational need for respect.* I feel respected when you value my thoughts and ideas and consider me a person of worth (1 Peter 2:17).

- *The relational need for security.* I feel secure when you take steps to remove the fear of loss or want in my life, or when you let me know that no matter what our relationship is solid (1 John 4:18).

- *The relational need for affection.* I feel close to you when you communicate care for me through endearing words and appropriate physical touch (Romans 12:10).

- *The relational need for encouragement.* I feel encouraged by you when you inspire me and urge me forward to a positive goal (Hebrews 10:24).

Wouldn't it be great to know which of those relational needs your kids need most? Every one of us has all those needs to varying degrees and it's important relationally to have them met. Yet it seems some of those needs are a higher priority to each of us individually. For example, my son, Sean, has a high need for respect, while my daughter Heather has a high need for attention. Dottie has a high need for support, and I have a high need for appreciation. It's really helpful to know the two or three highest relational needs of each of your children, yourself, and your wife, and then share what they are with one another. It's a real thrill when families begin to consciously take steps to meet each other's relational needs.

To help you identify those needs in order of their priority in your own life and the lives of your family members, I have provided a very useful tool. It's called the "Relational Needs Assessment Inventory"; you can find it in the back of this book. This testing tool is provided by David Ferguson and the Great Commandment Network and is an excellent way to get a handle on what relational needs are the most important to you and your family members.

To get my kids accustomed to recognizing and meeting the relational needs of others I involved them in my efforts to meet Dottie's needs. That way I was able to be a model for them, but it also gave them an opportunity to actually meet a relational need in the life of their mother. Take a birthday, for example. You no doubt have birthday celebrations every year for each of your kids. That's a perfect time to meet one of their top needs. Make sure your kids know you want to meet one of their relational needs when you celebrate the anniversary of their birth. Later, explain that because they have had a need met they can meet a need in others, specifically by celebrating their mom's birthday.

What I would do was secretly gather my kids together to help me make plans for Dottie's birthday. I'd say, "Kids, your mother's birthday is coming up and I need your help. What can we do to let Mom know how much we love and support her?"

In one of these secret meetings Kelly said, "We could take her to the beach because Mom loves the beach."

"I've got an idea," Sean announced. "Mom loves spaghetti—we could fix her a spaghetti dinner."

"I have a better idea," Katie chimed in. "Why don't we have a spaghetti picnic dinner at the beach?"

It was great engaging my kids this way because I was teaching them to meet a relational need in their mom just like they had one of their needs met at their own birthday celebrations. Each of them would write a special note of love and support in the birthday card we got Dottie. I let them know they had received a lot of love and support from their mom and now they were giving some of that back.

Take steps to show attention (care) to your kids and demonstrate acceptance, appreciation, support, encouragement, respect, security, comfort, approval, and affection toward them. But go further. Get them involved with you in meeting those same needs in the life of their mother. Ask them for their creative ideas and include them in actually meeting her relational needs along with you.

A Healthy Love Relationship Involves a Choice

It was a long time ago, but I vividly remember the words of the minister when he asked me: "Will you, Joslin David, take Dorothy Ann to be your wedded wife? To have and to hold from this day forward: for better, for worse; for richer, for poorer; in sickness or in health; to love and to cherish 'til death do you part?"

The end of that ceremony wasn't the conclusion of my marriage to Dottie. It was the beginning. A loving relationship, especially a marriage, isn't a destination; it is a relational journey sealed by a covenant of love. You see, loving someone actually involves a choice. I made a choice to be committed to Dottie, and that choice was a conscious decision to remain true to her and deepen my love for her for as long as I lived. Choosing to love my wife exclusively is what faithfulness and devotion is all about in a marriage relationship. Of course not every relationship we form with others is necessarily for a lifetime. Some friendships may drift apart for various reasons, but if you want a relationship to last it does require a conscious choice made repeatedly.

Let your kids know that love isn't simply a feeling or an emotional urge. Love is grounded in a covenant to be there for the other person regardless of the circumstances. Take advantage of your own wedding anniversaries to share that your marriage relationship is one of those meant to be for life. Occasionally make your wedding anniversary a family celebration. Let your kids know that faithfulness in your marriage is a choice and that you are constantly choosing to love your wife with a pure and exclusive love.

Take advantage of attending weddings with your kids too. Convey that loving relationships that last are those in which people make a choice—a solemn promise—to be true and faithful to each other.

Today it seems promises are easily broken, vows are only for the moment, and relationships are only for as long as the feelings are felt. Explain that is not God's design for marriage. Let your kids know that when a married couple commits to love with his kind of faithful love, the relationship is meant to last a lifetime.

A committed marital relationship that lasts is God's idea. All healthy love relationships are his idea, and they are other-focused and lovingly meet the needs of others. That is what Commitment #6 is all about—doing your best to impart God's way of forming healthy love relationships.

9

I Will Do My Best to Instruct on How to Know Right from Wrong

Aaron, I promised you that this wouldn't be like all those other 'talks' we've had," his dad began. "I honestly don't want to yell at you anymore."

Silence descended quickly on the room, punctuated by a sniffle from Marci, Aaron's mother. His dad, Rick, was confronting his 17-year-old son, who had been arrested for shoplifting at the local electronics store.

"I just want some answers," Rick continued. He began to draw his son out, asking questions.

"How do you feel after being arrested for shoplifting?"

"I don't know."

"Do you feel guilty?"

"No."

"Because you don't think it's wrong?"

"No. I guess I feel sorta bad."

"Why?"

"I don't know."

"Don't you know what you did was wrong?" Rick pressed.

They continued as Marci listened. At times, as she inspected Aaron's face and features, her son seemed like a stranger to her. At other times, she saw the little boy who would crawl up on her lap as she read him bedtime stories. The transformation from their little boy to a young man had not been easy for Rick and Marci.

The conversation turned, and Aaron was speaking.

"Why do *you* think it's so wrong?" he asked his dad, leaning forward and suddenly showing interest in the conversation.

Rick flashed him a puzzled look. "What do you mean?"

"Why is it so wrong? I took one measly camera, that's all. The last video camera I got from them never did work right. They owed me another camera but wouldn't give it to me. What's so wrong about taking what's owed you?"

"I can't believe this," Rick said. Aaron rolled his eyes. He slumped back against the couch and crossed his arms.

"Aaron," Rick answered abruptly, "your mother and I have tried to teach you honesty from day one. And it is so disappointing that you can't see that stealing is wrong."

"Who's stealing?" Aaron snapped. "I'm sure not. That store is the one stealing from the pockets of its customers every day. They're the ones who need to be arrested."

Rick fidgeted. He was beginning to lose his temper. "You know good and well you had no right to take that camera no matter what the store does to their customers. We've taught you better than that, Aaron Michael!"

Marci, seated beside Rick, responded to the anger in his voice by pressing on his arm firmly.

"Look," he said, an edge still in his voice. "Taking something from a store without paying for it is wrong, period, regardless of their business practices."

"Why?" Aaron persisted.

"What do you mean, 'Why?'" Rick shot back. "It's wrong! Some things are just wrong, dead wrong. And you and I both know what you did was wrong."

Aaron's voice rose in reaction. "Well, you may think it's wrong, but I don't. You're entitled to your opinion, and I'm entitled to mine. None of my friends think I did a thing wrong. The party in the wrong here is that store." He rose from the couch and began walking out of the room.

"You get back here right now, young man," Rick demanded.

"I've got to get ready for soccer," he announced from the top of the stairway.

Marci pressed Rick on the arm again.

"You promised him this 'talk' would be different." Her voice was steady, but not loud.

Rick leaned back in his chair, closed his eyes, and wondered how his boy's moral compass had gotten so far off the mark.

Rick and Marci want what you and I want—we want our kids to believe that certain things are right and other things are wrong, so they can make right moral choices in life. This dad knows his son has made the wrong choice but feels helpless to convince him otherwise. What we dads want to know is this—how do we instruct our kids to determine what is truly right from what is truly wrong so they can make the right moral choices?

We all know instinctively that some things are right and some things are wrong. Let Aaron discover, for example, that his soccer shoes were stolen from his school locker and he'll feel wronged. He wouldn't argue that the thief is entitled to his opinion of right and wrong; he would appeal to an objective sense of justice because he would claim that he had suffered an injustice. In so doing, of course, he would appeal to a moral law that he believes everyone—not just he—ought to follow.

In Aaron's opinion his actions were justified because the electronics store didn't treat him or other people fairly. So in effect his "moral law" made it okay to steal. In fact, the majority of our kids today believe it's okay to steal, lie, or cheat depending on the circumstance. According to them, what is wrong in one situation may be right in another. So how do you teach your kids right from wrong when they're surrounded by people who believe that "moral law" changes based on the circumstance?

Two Models of Truth

In today's culture there are two distinct models for knowing when something is right and when something is wrong. Each model affects how we see life—our worldview—and each represents a radically different perspective:

- *Model #1:* What is right or wrong is defined by God for everyone; it is objective and universal.

- *Model #2:* What is right or wrong is defined by the individual; it is subjective and situational.

The first model acknowledges that God—not humans—is central, that he is the source of all things, and that he rules over all. He is the repository of truth, the author and judge of all that is right and wrong.

The second model, on the other hand, places the individual in control of moral matters. Because the standard resides within the individual, it is particular to that specific person (subjective) and the circumstance he or she is in (situational). In other words, each person considers himself or herself the judge of whatever is true and determines individually what is right or wrong.

The vast majority of kids, even in Christian homes, work from Model #2. If you have teenagers they probably hold to this viewpoint or at least have been greatly influenced by the subjective and situational model. To move our kids solidly to the first model we must help them determine what actually makes right, right—and wrong, wrong. And to do that we must establish a standard for right and wrong—the original standard.

Establishing the Original Standard

In the town of Sèvres, France, a suburb of Paris, is the headquarters of the International Bureau of Weights and Measures, an organization that standardizes units of measure. The bureau establishes standards for metric measurements and maintains a reliable standard for physical measurements around the world.

If I wanted to obtain the most precise measurement possible, I would refer to the standard they maintain. If I wanted to be absolutely certain that the millimeter divisions on my ruler were accurate, I would compare them against the bureau's standards. If I wanted to know whether the bottle of Diet Coke in my refrigerator contained exactly two liters of liquid, I could check it against the Bureau's measurements.

Now, suppose you and I had a dispute about a length of wood I had cut for you. I measured it and told you it was one meter long; you measured it with your own meterstick and pronounced that it was less than one meter. How could we determine who was right? We could appeal to the standard—there exists an objective and universal standard for measurements in Sèvres. To determine the validity of our individual measurements, we need only refer to the original.

That is just what our kids need. They need to be convinced that a standard exists for settling claims about moral knowledge, a standard for right and wrong that is universal and that exists outside ourselves.

As we must do when measuring lengths, we must also do in discerning moral right from wrong. So to determine truth, we first ask, *How does it compare to the original?* The first step in this process, then, is to test what is thought to be right and true against the original. Webster defines truth, in part, as "fidelity to an original or standard."

The question is, of course, what—or who—is the original?

This is where God must be made part of the discussion—because it is impossible to arrive at an objective and universal standard of morality without him in the picture. If an objective standard of truth and morality exists, it cannot be the product of the human mind or it will not be objective; it must be the product of another mind. And if a universal rule of right and wrong exists, it must transcend individual experience or it will not be universal; it must be above us all. And universal truth, by definition, must be something—or Someone—that is common to all humanity, to all creation.

Those things—those requirements for a standard of truth and morality—are met only in one being—God. Just as he is awesome in his holiness (see chapter 6), he is the source of all truth. "He is the Rock," Moses said, "his work is perfect…a God of truth and without iniquity, just and right is he" (Deuteronomy 32:4 KJV). You see, it is his nature and character that define truth and what is right from wrong. He defines what is right for all people, for all times, in all places. But truth is not something he decides; it is something he *is*.

The basis of everything we call moral, the source of every good thing, is the eternal God who is outside us, above us, and beyond us. The apostle James wrote, "Every good and perfect gift is from above, coming down from the Father of the heavenly lights, who does not change like shifting shadows" (James 1:17 NIV).

A lot of parents are like Rick in our opening story. They think, *Some things are just wrong, dead wrong.* But trying to help our kids develop firm convictions about right and wrong with such reasoning goes nowhere; we must equip them with a sturdy framework of biblical reasoning. We must ingrain within them the understanding that the reason we have this concept that some things are right and some things are wrong is because there exists a Creator, Yahweh God, and he is a righteous God.

The reason we think there are such things as "fair" and "unfair" is because our Maker is a *just* God.

The reason love is a virtue and hatred a vice is because the God who formed us is a God of *love*.

The reason honesty is right and deceit is wrong is because God is *true*.

The reason chastity is moral and promiscuity is immoral is because God is *pure* and *faithful*.

And the reason so many of our kids can't distinguish between the real and the counterfeit, between truth and error, between what's moral and what's immoral, is because they are not measuring their attitudes and actions against the original. We all have been influenced by the cultural shift away from God as the center of all things. Our culture has rejected the source of truth and has tried to come up with its own ideas about right and wrong.

Rick's pitiful response to his son's "why" questions is typical of so many who measure right and wrong by their own ideas rather than God's character. It's not enough to say, "You and I both know that what you did was wrong!" It's not what *I* know, nor what *you* know, that makes a thing wrong; it's *what God is* that makes it wrong.

Challenge Their Thinking

I made a practice of having discussions with my teenage kids in order to shape and sharpen their thinking. When I came home after a trip, I'd often take the kids out for breakfast. As I drove to the restaurant (or while we were all munching on our bacon and eggs), I'd suggest a situation in which we might be called upon to make a moral decision. The kids and I would discuss it and try to decide what course of action to take, based on God's character and his law. The idea was to challenge their thinking and lead them to discover that morality is morality because of God.

First, we had to determine what law or commandment from God applied, but the important thing was to see how that law actually originated and grew out of his character and how it reflected his love and care for us. My purpose was to acquaint my children with the kind of God we serve, not just the kind of laws we follow, and to instill in them a foundation for evaluating, on an objective basis, what truths were universal—right for all people, for all times, in all places.

At one point, I took my 13-year-old daughter and my 17-year-old son and his girlfriend to see Steven Spielberg's 1993 movie *Schindler's List*. It seemed everyone was talking about it at the time. It won seven Academy Awards, including Best Picture and Best Director. It was about a German businessman named Oskar Schindler, who saved the lives of more than a thousand mostly Polish-Jewish refugees during the Nazi Holocaust.

As we left the theater, we were surrounded by a somber crowd, many of whom were commenting on the atrocities inflicted upon the Jews by the Nazis. I turned to my son.

"Sean," I said, "do you believe the Holocaust was wrong—morally wrong?"

He answered quickly. "Yes."

Then, as we got into the car to travel to a nearby town for dinner, I pursued the matter. "Almost everyone walking out of that theater would say the Holocaust was wrong," I said. "But what basis would they have for making that judgment? Could they answer *why* it was wrong?"

I could see the wheels of three teenage minds spinning as I continued. "Most people in America subscribe to a view of morality called 'cultural ethics.' In other words, they believe that whatever is acceptable in that culture is moral; if the majority of people say a thing is 'right,' then it is right."

At about that time, we arrived at the restaurant, and we continued the discussion over dinner. "That's why many Americans will say that abortion is okay, because the majority of Americans—and Congress and the Supreme Court—have accepted it. If the majority thinks it's okay, it must be okay, right?

"But there's a problem with that," I explained. "If that is true, then how can we say the 'aborting' of six million Jews in the Holocaust was wrong? In fact, the Nazis offered that very argument as a defense at the Nuremberg Trials. They argued, 'How can you come from another culture and condemn what we did when we acted according to what our culture said was acceptable?' In condemning them, the tribunal said that there is something beyond culture, above culture, that determines right and wrong."

I also went on to explain that most of what people call morality today is simply pragmatism. "*If we don't condemn what the Nazis did,* people reason within themselves, *what's to stop someone from doing it to us?* And they're right, of course," I told them. "They recognize the need for objective morality, but they cannot arrive at a true moral code—because they refuse to acknowledge the original."

Finally, after about two hours of discussion, I thought it was time to guide my kids to a discovery. "Do you know *why* what you saw tonight was wrong?"

"I know it was wrong," Sean ventured, "but I don't know why."

"There is a truth," I said, "that is outside me, above our family, and beyond any human—a truth about murder that originates in the person of God. Murder is wrong because there is a God and that God is the giver and preserver of life, the one who said, 'It is good,' and commanded us to protect life and not to commit murder." That night I reinforced in my children and their friend that God is the original life-giver and is the one with authority over life—he has the right to give life and to take life. Without him as the standard, there can be no universal moral guidelines.

The 4-Cs Process

The reasoning I communicated to my kids applies to all other ethical issues as well. As mentioned, lying and stealing are wrong because God is true. Justice is right because God is just. Hatred is wrong because God is love. Forgiveness is right because God is mercy. Sexual immorality is wrong because God is faithful and pure. These things are right or wrong, not because society or the church agrees with them or frowns on them, but because they are either contrary to or consistent with the nature and character of God.

A couple years after I discussed *Schindler's List* with my kids I launched a campaign called "Right from Wrong." And during that time my publishing team worked with me to create an easy-to-use process to teach kids how to determine what is morally right from wrong. We called it the "4-Cs Process." Hundreds of thousands of families have used it and still use it to help their kids determine what is truly right and what is truly wrong.

Let's use Rick and Aaron as an example of what this dad could have done to help his son determine how taking from even a disreputable electronics store was wrong—before he actually stole the camera.

The 4-Cs Process is made up of four decision-making steps:

1. *Consider* the choice;
2. *Compare* it to God;
3. *Commit* to God's way; and
4. *Count* on God's protection and provision.

1. Consider the Choice

In a single day each of us makes literally scores of choices. Most of them are almost automatic. We choose what time to get up in the morning, what clothes to wear, what to eat, what route to take to work or school, where to park, and so on. We take little time considering these choices.

But when it comes to moral choices, we need to pause and realize we are at a crossroads. The choices we make—to be less than honest, to advance a flirtation to the next level, or for our kids to enhance their scores by "borrowing" someone else's answers—are often made without considering the gravity of what we are really doing. To make right moral choices, we must first pause long enough to remind ourselves that we are facing an opportunity for a right or wrong decision.

Let's assume Aaron had told his dad about the video camera he bought that never did work right and about his frustration with the store's response not to make it right. How could Rick have guided his son to the realization that taking a camera from a less-than-reputable store was still wrong using the 4-Cs Process?

"I took the camera back, Dad, and they won't do anything to fix it unless they charge me," Aaron laments. "They say I must have messed it up, but I didn't. I feel like taking a new camera when they're not looking so I can replace this crummy one. They've gotta pay somehow, Dad."

"You're right, son," Rick responds, "they are not doing right by you. But you need to pause a minute to realize this is a time to consider the choice. There is a right decision here to make and a wrong one. And you want to make the right choice, because choices do have consequences."

2. Compare the Choice to God

A long time ago one of the two first humans made a wrong choice in part because she didn't compare it to God. Eve seemed to pause long enough to realize she was about to make a right or wrong choice. But she failed to compare her decision to her Creator. That is what healthy relationships do—they take the other person into consideration. In this case, was Eve to believe God had her best interest at heart in denying her a certain fruit? Or would she believe he was trying to selfishly keep her from becoming sovereign over her life as he was over his?

What Eve failed to do was to take God into consideration and compare her attitude and action to him, which would have meant looking at the choice in relation to his commands, which were in fact in her best interest. This, of course, would have required that she believe that he was her universal standard for right—not herself.

Using this approach Rick could have said to Aaron:

"Son, I know it doesn't seem fair. The store sold you a defective camera and they won't make it right. They are in fact being dishonest with you."

"You're right, Dad," Aaron responds. "For once you're really right."

Rick laughs and continues. "We could say since the store won't own up to their dishonesty we are justified in making them own up—we can then take what is properly ours, right?"

"Right on," Aaron replies. "And besides they've got so many cameras they won't even miss it if we lift one from them."

"This all may sound good on the surface," Rick says to his son. "But what we are doing is justifying our actions based on what *we* think is right, rather than looking to God, who defines what honesty and dishonesty really is."

What Rick is doing here is directing his son to the original standard for what constitutes honesty. Aaron was rationalizing that it wasn't actually dishonest to steal from someone who owes another person. But when we take it on ourselves to rationalize this way, we are actually usurping God's role as the sovereign arbiter, based on his character and nature, of what is right or wrong. God's Word says,

- Do not steal.
- Do not lie.
- Do not deceive one another...
- Do not defraud or rob your neighbor (Leviticus 19:11-13 NIV).

God's commands to be honest come out of his nature, and his nature is true and right. Scripture states that "even if everyone else is a liar, God is true" (Romans 3:4). By his very nature he is a God of integrity and because of this "it is impossible for God to lie" (Hebrews 6:18). So when we compare ourselves to him we are admitting that he is sovereign; he is the one who defines what is right and what is wrong regarding honesty and every other moral action. When we make our moral decision in light of the character of God, our choice becomes crystal clear—in this example, we are to commit to being honest even when we are wronged by a dishonest business.

3. Commit to God's Way

Committing to God's way is easier said than done. It means we have to admit we are not the ruler over our lives—he is. The present-day concept of deciding what is "right for you" appeals to so many people because it puts us in charge. It permits us to justify our attitudes and actions regardless of how they compare to God's nature and character. Granting ourselves the capacity to decide our own morality feels independent and empowering. And that is not easy to resist.

"Aaron, it may feel like justice is served to take a camera from the store," Rick continues. "But it's never just to go against God's standard of honesty. If you were to take what you felt was rightfully yours while the store wasn't looking, it would be deceitful and still wrong. You would be in effect setting yourself up as judge, jury, and executioner, and God says that is his role: 'It is mine to avenge; I will repay' (Deuteronomy 32:35 niv). He tells us to 'not seek revenge or bear a grudge' (Leviticus 19:18).

"But, Dad, it's still not fair," Aaron protests.

"You're right, it's not fair," Rick agrees. "But there are things in life that are not fair that we must leave in God's hands. Jesus, for example, was certainly treated unfairly, yet the Bible says, 'He did not retaliate when he was insulted, nor threaten revenge when he suffered. He left his case in the hands of God, who always judges fairly'" (1 Peter 2:23).

"And," Rick added, "you can count on it, God will honor you for doing the right thing and leaving the future of the electronics store up to the owner. Scripture tells us, 'Even if you suffer for doing what is right, God will reward you for it'" (1 Peter 3:14).

4. Count on God's Protection and Provision

When we humbly admit God's sovereignty and lovingly seek to please him, not only can we begin to see clearly the distinctions between right and wrong; we can also begin to count on his protection and provision.

This doesn't mean that everything will be rosy; in fact, God says bluntly that we may suffer for righteousness' sake. But even such suffering has rewards. Living according to his way brings many spiritual blessings, like freedom from guilt, a clear conscience, and the joy of his smile upon our lives.

We can also enjoy many physical, emotional, psychological, and relational benefits when we commit to his ways. Of course, his protection and provision should not be the primary motivation for obeying him; we should obey him simply because we love him and trust him. But the practical and spiritual benefits of obedience certainly provide powerful encouragement for choosing right and rejecting wrong.

Rick had the opportunity to help Aaron realize that adhering to God's standard of honesty would bring protection and provision to him on at least four levels. Aligning ourselves with God's standard of honesty...

- protects us from guilt and provides for a clear conscience and unbroken fellowship with him
- protects us from shame and provides for a sense of accomplishment
- protects us from the cycle of deceit and provides for a reputation of integrity
- protects us from ruined relationships and provides for trusting relationships

If there is any secret to making the right choices in life it is in having the deep conviction that God always has your best interest at heart. Instill within your kids that he is a good God who loves them beyond their comprehension. And when they believe that with their whole heart, they can obey his commands to be honest, live sexually pure, love and respect others, show mercy, forgive, exhibit self-control, and so on. Being obedient isn't simply about obligation and duty—it comes from a "God who is passionate about his relationship with [them]" (Exodus 34:14 NLT). Embrace that truth in your own life—and instill it in the life of your kids.*

* For additional help, tap into the Right from Wrong resources our team has developed with me. There are small-group courses for teens and children, along with books. Simply go to www.josh.org.

10

I Will Do My Best to
Teach How to Honor God's Design for Sex

She tapped me on the shoulder. "Mr. McDowell, thank you so much for what you shared. I've never heard anything like this before."

I had just finished a seminar talk on the "Bare Facts About Sex" and this mother wanted to let me know she was going to "apply" the message. She went on to say, "I've got to have my husband give our son 'the talk.'"

Without trying to sound alarmed, I replied, "How old is your son?" She said, "Thirteen." I had to control my surprise and astonishment. "You haven't been interacting with your son before this about sexual issues?" I asked. She said, "Oh, no...we haven't had the chance."

The "big talk" is a relic of the past. And it never should have been endorsed in the first place. The *Journal of Family Issues* reported that "just half of adolescents feel they had one 'good talk' about sexuality during the past year with their mothers—and only one third with their fathers."[1]

Dad, sexual issues should not be taught to your kids in a "big talk." It should instead be an unfolding process with information given out in little chunks at a time. Deal with issues and opportunities as they arise. Most young children cannot absorb or grasp more than just short conversations. They can and will forget the "big talk" very quickly.

The best sex education is 30 seconds here, 1 minute there, 10 seconds here, 2 minutes and 45 seconds there, and so on, starting as young as possible. When something comes up, step in, address it, and step back. Don't make a big deal out of it. In our family, about half of all the conversations we had with our kids about sex were no longer than about two minutes.

For most kids, the topic of sex comes in stages. They very seldom open up all at once. They open up as the result of an ongoing dialogue as they mature and grow older. Be ready, though, because when they do open up, it can often happen at the most inopportune times and places.

"For the life of me," says my grown son, Sean, "I cannot remember a distinct first time when I talked about sex with my parents. And I think that's because in my family, it was just a natural part of life. It's not that we talked about it all the time—but when it came up at the dinner table or in the car or before bed we simply talked about it. It was just like other topics—just a normal part of our conversation. So there was no one distinct time where I got the 'big talk.'" [2]

Explain the Purpose for Sex

If one big talk is not a good idea, then just what are the little talks to be about? As a dad who wants their kids to honor God's design for sex, one of the things you want your kids to understand is what sex is all about. You want them to understand God's purpose for sex, and you want them to learn that from you.

Explain That Sex Is for Togetherness

It doesn't take long for your kids to realize they are attracted to the opposite sex. God created male and female with this natural attraction for one another. "This explains," the Bible says, "why a man leaves his father and mother and is joined to his wife, and the two are united into one" (Genesis 2:24). Our desire and need for intimacy in relationship is rooted in the image of God as one (see Deuteronomy 6:4). Marriage and marital sex between a man and a woman reflects his nature of oneness and unity. Sexuality is a beautiful gift from him that gives humans the capacity for an intimate, loving relationship.

Some guys have grown up believing *sex* is a dirty word. And they have carried that distorted view into their marriages. If so, it's difficult to understand how a "dirty" thing can bring an intimate connection with their wife. Yet that is part of God's design and purpose for sex.

This truth has even been confirmed on a biological level. Researchers have discovered a hormone called *oxytocin*, nicknamed the "cuddle hormone." Oxytocin is a chemical your brain releases during sex and the activity leading up to it. When this chemical is released, it fosters feelings of caring, trust, and deep affection. Yet relational intimacy isn't fully achieved by simply engaging in a physical sex act. Human sexuality involves every aspect of a person's being—physically, emotionally, spiritually, and relationally. And sex is meant to connect us on every level.

However, most of our kids are confused over what sex is all about. Many think that sex is there to simply make them feel physically close to their boyfriend or girlfriend. Sure—sex gives you a physical sense of closeness for a brief moment, but one of its real purposes is to bring every dimension of a couple together spiritually, emotionally, and relationally for a lifetime. That is why Jesus said, "Since they [a married couple] are no longer two but one, let no one split apart what God has joined together" (Matthew 19:6). So until a man or woman is ready to commit to a lifetime of intimacy, they should not be engaging in an act that is designed for that very thing.

Dad, the one thing you need to make clear to your kids is that sex—that attraction between the opposite sex—is God's beautiful gift to create an intimate bond with the person they marry. It's not something that is dirty even though some people misuse it and distort his purpose for it. Just because a destructive culture distorts a beautiful thing doesn't mean you act as though it's a plague. Lift up sex and human sexuality to the high level that God designed it. After all, it came from him—he created us as sexual beings.

Explain That Sex Is for Pleasure

God created sex and sexual relations as a bonding agent to deeply connect a man and a woman together spiritually, emotionally, relationally, and physically for a lifetime. But he didn't create this "bonding agent" as a one-time event. The "urge to merge" can be felt as frequently and as often as our appetite for food, perhaps even more so for some.

Intimacy is a very important factor of sex, but engaging in marital sex for sheer pleasure is another. Sex should be a blast for a married man and woman who commit to loving one another for as long as possible.

Let your kids know in appropriate ways that God meant sexual relations to be enjoyable. One of the things I did as our kids were growing up was to let them know how much Dottie and I enjoyed each other. Of course kids don't want to mentally envision their parents' sexual encounters. But I let my kids know that sexual relations were designed to be a beautiful and enjoyable experience when expressed in the context of marriage. And in very subtle ways I let them know Dottie and I enjoyed God's gift a great deal. And by the way, if you need scriptural reinforcements that God wants sex to be enjoyed within the context of marriage, check out the Song of Songs (Song of Solomon), chapter 7.

Explain That Sex Is for Procreation

One of the first things God said to the first couple, Adam and Eve, was, "Be fruitful and multiply" (Genesis 1:28). Now that has to be one of the most enjoyable commands to ever fulfill! And without fulfilling this procreation command, the human race would not continue.

At the beginning of that verse it says, "Then God blessed them and said, 'Be fruitful and multiply...'" (Genesis 1:28). The result of having children is clearly a blessing. Solomon said, "Grandchildren are the crowning glory of the aged; parents are the pride of their children" (Proverbs 17:6).

Perhaps there is no greater thrill than to realize that your intimate expression of love for your spouse has created a precious life that will forever be known as your son or daughter. Sure, there are challenges to birthing and raising a child these days. But what an awesome privilege and blessing it is to have a family! Let your kids know that God's gift of sex is what brought them into this world.

Our children need to understand how God wants sex to bless their lives and relationships. They need to understand its purpose. But if they are to use it right, they also must understand "the rules of engagement."[3] God has a very specific design for sex—a way it is to be used—and when we follow that design we enjoy its benefits. But if we fail to follow his guidelines we can suffer devastating results. That is why you want to teach your kids how to honor his design.

There Is a Design for Sex

Have you ever tried to take a pet fish on a walk, or grow a palm tree at the North Pole, or simply screw in a Phillips head screw with a conventional screwdriver? You will have problems all the way around. Why? Because fish were not created to take walks. They were designed to live in water, not on land. And if a fish is going to enjoy its life as it was meant to be enjoyed, then it has to live where it was created and meant to live—in water.

Palm trees were meant to flourish in perpetually warm weather. They are tropical trees. If they are to live as they were meant to live, they have to stay away from cold climates like the North Pole. Even a simple task like screwing a Phillips screw into a wall becomes hard when you use the wrong screwdriver. If machines, plants, and animals are going to experience maximum function they have to exist according to their design. It's just that simple.

Your kids need to understand that because sex is from God it has a design. Sex is a fantastic gift to increasingly deepen a married couple's love life, to bring joy and physical pleasure into their relationship, and to create a loving family of one or more children. If you respect and honor sex for how it was meant to be used, then—wow, sex is one of the best things God created.

But how do we really honor his design for sex? If sex is for togetherness, pleasure, and procreation then how do we maximize it to enjoy all its benefits? God gives us the answer in the protective boundaries he has placed around sex. As dads, we want to teach our kids to honor his design for sex by following the rules or boundaries for maximum sex.

Teach the Boundaries for Sexual Morality

In earlier chapters I've talked a lot about how God's commands are meant for our best interest. It certainly is true when it comes to our sex lives. The do's and don'ts regarding sexual behavior form guidelines or boundaries that we can clearly understand and live within. And the reason God established these boundaries is to provide for us and protect us. Check out Psalm 145. It describes him as a gracious provider and protector.

But to experience the protection and provision God has planned for us requires that we honor the boundaries and prohibition signs for sexual behavior. In other words, we must avoid sexual immorality.

In biblical terms, sexual immorality is all sex that occurs outside of a marriage between one man and one woman (extramarital and premarital sex). Scripture declares,

- "You must abstain from...sexual immorality" (Acts 15:29).
- "Run from sexual sin!" (1 Corinthians 6:18).
- "We must not engage in sexual immorality" (1 Corinthians 10:8).
- "Among you there must not be even a hint of sexual

immorality…because these are improper for God's holy people" (Ephesians 5:3 NIV).

- "God's will is for you to be holy, so stay away from all sexual sin" (1 Thessalonians 4:3).

Respecting the boundaries of sexual morality and the "stop" signs for extramarital and premarital sex does bring protection and provision. Here are just a few examples:

Protection from	Provision for
guilt	spiritual rewards
unplanned pregnancy	optimum atmosphere for child-raising
sexually transmitted diseases	peace of mind
sexual insecurity	trust
emotional distress	true intimacy

Experiencing those benefits definitely maximizes a person's sex life in marriage. For example, when I was a young man I made a clear choice to wait until the loving commitment of marriage before experiencing sexual relations. That commitment meant I would remain sexually celibate until I met and married the woman of my dreams and then remain faithful. Dottie made that same commitment. And because we both were obedient to God's commands regarding sex, we have been protected from feelings of guilt and have enjoyed an uninterrupted relationship with him.

We have never had to go through the heartache of a pregnancy before marriage. Consequently, we have not experienced the heart-wrenching ordeal of planning an adoption or struggling with getting married before we were ready because of pregnancy.

We have been protected from the fear that any sexually transmitted disease might come into our marriage bed.

We have been protected from the sexual insecurity that can come from being compared to past sexual lovers one's spouse may have had. And consequently, we have experienced the provision of trust in our relationship.

We have been protected from the emotional distress that premarital sex can bring and the feelings of betrayal that an extramarital affair can cause. As a result we have enjoyed relational intimacy together unobstructed by breaches of trust or ghosts from the past.

Sex as God designed it was meant to be lived within the context of healthy boundaries—prohibitions before marriage and fidelity after marriage. Following God's design then allows a couple to experience the beauty of sex as it was meant to be experienced. But it is vitally important that your kids understand what these boundaries are and be able to identify them by name. Because these boundaries and limits are what make the "no" such a positive answer—and they are the very reason sex is maximized when we live within them.

The Boundary of Purity

The Bible says, "Marriage should be honored by all, and the marriage bed kept pure" (Hebrews 13:4 NIV). "God's will is for you to be holy, so stay away from all sexual sin. Then each of you will control his own body and live in holiness and honor—not in lustful passion…God has called us to live holy lives, not impure lives" (1 Thessalonians 4:3-5,7).

Purity is God's boundary that provides for a maximum sex life and protects us from the negative consequences of sexual immorality. But what does it mean to be pure?

Have you ever had a candy bar that identified itself on the wrapper as "pure milk chocolate"? What about a jar of honey? Some labels read, "Pure honey—no artificial sweeteners." *Pure* describing chocolate or honey means there is no foreign substance to contaminate it or to keep it from being and tasting like authentic chocolate or real honey.

To be pure sexually is to "live according to God's original design," without allowing anything to come in to ruin his authentic, perfect plan for sex. Sex was designed to be expressed between one husband and one wife. To have more than one sexual partner would be to bring a foreign substance into the relationship, and that relationship would cease to be pure. If you were to drop a dirty pebble into a glass of pure water, it would become adulterated—impure. A glass of water without any impurities in it is an unadulterated glass of water. God wants our sex lives to be unadulterated.

Let your kids know that God designed sex to be experienced within an unbroken circle, a pure union between two virgins entering into an exclusive relationship. That pure union can be broken even *before* marriage, if one or both of the partners has not kept the marriage bed pure by waiting to have sex until it can be done in the purity of a husband-wife relationship.

Where did sexual purity come from? From the very character of God himself. God says, "Be holy, for I am holy" (1 Peter 1:16 NASB). "All who have this hope [of being like Christ when he returns] in him purify themselves, just as he [God] is pure" (1 John 3:3 NIV). God by nature is holy and pure. "There is no evil in him" (Psalm 92:15). Help your kids understand that if they remain sexually pure before marriage and after marriage, they will enjoy the protection and provision of sex and experience it as God meant it to be experienced.

The Boundary of Faithfulness

The seventh commandment is "You must not commit adultery" (Exodus 20:14). Jesus made the point that once a man and woman are united as one in marriage they are not to commit adultery but remain faithful to one another. He said, "Let no one split apart what God has joined together" (Mark 10:9). God told Israel, "I hate divorce!…so guard your heart; do not be unfaithful to your wife" (Malachi 2:16).

What couples do at their wedding is commit to be faithful to one another…"to have and to hold, from this day forward: for better, for worse; for richer, for poorer; in sickness and in health; to love and to cherish 'til death do us part. And hereto I pledge you my faithfulness." Perhaps nothing is more rewarding than to sense that someone loves you more than any other and will devote themselves to you for life. Faithfulness is God's boundary that provides for a maximum sex life and protects us from the negative consequences of sexual immorality.

I have traveled away from home for most of my married life. I have had more than one opportunity to be unfaithful to Dottie. But in over 40 years of marriage I have resisted temptation and demonstrated loyalty, faithfulness, and devoted commitment to only one love-and-sex relationship in my life. And that of course is with Dottie. That means the world to her. It deepens her sense of worth, and it gives her security and tells her she is loved. Of all the more than 3 billion women on this planet she is the one and only lover for me.

We were created by God with the desire and longing to be that "one and only" to someone else. That desire came directly from the very nature of God himself. "Understand…that the LORD your God is indeed God," Moses told the Israelites. "He is the faithful God who keeps his covenant for a thousand generations" (Deuteronomy 7:9).

Sex Within the Context of Love

Let your kids know that sex is to be lived within the boundaries of purity on one side and faithfulness on the other. What that does is provide the healthy context for a married couple's sexual relationship. And that context is love.

Most kids growing up in a Christian home have a moral standard. If you have a teenager he or she probably believes that kids having sex with anyone, anytime, is definitely wrong. And, of course, you should be proud he or she holds that view. But there's a catch.

Most kids from good churches and Christian families feel that it is somehow different if two people are in a committed relationship where "true love" is involved. Then engaging in sex before marriage seems justified because "love makes it right."

I shock many parents and church leaders when I say that I agree, in a way, with today's young people—I believe that true love *does* make it right. Now, you probably know where I'm going here because we have already defined love biblically in a previous chapter. The problem is, however, most young people have not defined love biblically and they are working from a counterfeit standard of love—one that says love permits sex without the boundaries of purity and fidelity.

As you remember, we defined love as making the security, happiness, and welfare of another person as important as your own. Let your kids know that they honor God's design for sex when they love another person like that and allow the boundaries of purity and faithfulness to guide their sex life. Help them to realize that obedience to God's instructions is meant to provide for their happiness and protects them from harm. Love—true love—will wait until marriage to engage in sex and remain pure and faithful after marriage. So in that respect, true love does make it right.

And where does this love originate? Of course, from God, "for God is love" (1 John 4:8). His definition of love is the kind that protects the loved one from harm and provides for his or her good. His love is giving and trusting, secure and safe, loyal and forever. And because true love's priority is to protect and provide for the one being loved, God's kind of love will not do things that are harmful to the security, happiness, and welfare of another person. [4]

A Conversation Here, a Conversation There

We started out by saying to avoid the "big talk" and go with an unfolding process that gives out information about sex in little chunks. In the chapter on God's way to form healthy love relationships we suggested using anniversaries and weddings as opportunities to talk about love and relationship. Those are good times to include a little chunk of information about God's design for sex too. Here are a few ways you can seize events, circumstances, and other resources to help you do your best to establish your kids in how to honor God's design for sex.

- *Celebrate anniversaries in front of your kids.* Wedding anniversaries are ideal times to let your kids know how faithfulness and purity have protected and provided for you in the areas we've discussed. Make your anniversary a family celebration. Let your kids know how much marital fidelity means to you. Tell them what the marriage commitment has done for your relationship. The more they see how your love, faithfulness, and purity have benefited your lives and theirs, the more impact it will have on them.

  Don't underestimate the ability of younger children (six, five, or even four years old, for example) to understand the principles of biblical love, sexual purity, and marital fidelity. You have an excellent opportunity to build a foundation for their sexual chastity by helping them understand these things. You can explain your love for your spouse by describing how your spouse is as important to you as your own body. You can explain your faithfulness in the form of promise-keeping. You can explain marital fidelity by saying, "That is why I live only with your mother and with no one else." Teach them early of your commitment to their mother and how you are exclusively devoted to her. Your modeling and teaching will pay off when their hormones start raging.

- *Take full advantage of weddings.* Go to weddings as a family and use those occasions to celebrate God's boundaries of faithfulness and purity. Make sure your kids understand a wedding's significance. Take time before and following the ceremony to emphasize the commitment the couple is making and their promise to be faithful for a lifetime. Get a copy of the marriage vows and read them together with your younger children. Teenagers may not respond favorably to reading them together, but you can make the time exciting to a child or pre-teen. Weddings are an ideal time to reinforce God's design for love and sex within the marriage commitment—and how that reflects the character of God.

• *Use opportunities presented by TV, news, and current affairs.* Take every opportunity to correct the warped portrayals of love and sex in the news and "entertainment" media. When you and your kids see something on television or in the movies that contradicts God's standard for love and sex, discuss the benefits and consequences of obeying his command. You may be surprised how insightful your youth are in detecting the benefits and consequences of people's actions once they begin to see life through the "lens" of God's design for sex.

• *Take advantage of the resources.* There are many books, CDs, and DVD courses designed to help you as a dad teach your kids a biblical perspective on sex. This chapter is drawn from a book written by Dottie and me entitled *Straight Talk with Your Kids About Sex.* This book offers detailed ways to talk to your kids about sex and teach them to honor God's design. I have also created a book, CD, and DVD series called The Bare Facts: The Truth about Sex, Love and Relationships.*

Take advantage of other resources. Go to your local Christian bookstore, order ministry catalogs, find out what your denomination offers—you may be surprised just how many excellent tools there are available to help you teach your kids God's design for sex.

---

* You can check these resources out at www.josh.org.

I Will Do My Best to
Present Why We Believe What We Believe

Marsha hugged her son as he prepared to leave. "It's been nice having you home again, honey," she said.

"Yeah, Greg," his father, Mike, echoed. "It really has been good." He stepped in for a hug. "I miss the weekends as a family, going to church and all. But I assume you've found a church home there in the college area by now, haven't you, son?"

Greg swung his backpack onto his shoulder. "Well, Dad, not really," he said hesitantly. "Being a freshman is tough, so I've been really busy."

Sarah, Greg's 16-year-old sister, handed him his shoulder bag. "Is college really that hard?"

"Well, I wouldn't say hard, really. You just keep busy, you know?"

Mike gently gripped Greg's shoulder. "If you're too busy to be in church, son, I think you might be too busy."

"Well," Greg responded, "your kind of church just isn't my thing anymore, Dad. I've got some friends and we get together once a week and that's enough for me."

"I'd rather do things with my friends too," Sarah added. "Church is a bore."

"Sarah!" Marsha said. "That's a terrible thing to say!"

"Well, it's true!" Sarah said.

"She's right, Mom," Greg said. "Church just doesn't cut it for me anymore."

"Honey, don't say that." Marsha touched her son on the arm. "That college isn't turning you against God, is it?"

"No, Mom," Greg chuckled, "I'm just rethinking a lot of things. God is still important to me—I just believe some different things from you guys, that's all." He adjusted the weight of the shoulder bag. "Hey, I've got to get going."

Greg moved on out the door as Sarah helped him with his things. Marsha and Mike stepped onto the porch and watched their son walk toward the car.

"We'll be praying for you, son," Mike called.

"Thanks, Dad," Greg responded with a chuckle.

Marsha and Mike watched in silence as he backed down the drive and waved to them as he drove away. "I hope we're not losing our son," Marsha said.

Mike nodded. "I hope we're not losing our son *and* our daughter." [1]

If I hear one dominant and recurring theme among the dads I come in contact with, it's the fear that Mike expressed above. It is the fear that you can raise your kids to embrace your Christian values and faith and then as they leave home and go off to college they will walk away from the true faith.

That concern is not just a phobia. Studies show that within ten years of entering adulthood, most teens professing to be Christian will walk away from the church and put whatever commitment they made to Christ on the shelf. [2] This doesn't mean that there's a good chance your kids will reject God outright and become atheists. That's not the case. Rather, they're adopting beliefs that are definitely not "the faith which was once for all handed down to the saints" (Jude 3 NASB).

A large portion of kids from good Christian homes today would echo Greg's remark to his dad: "God is still important to me—I just believe some different things than you." These differences, sometimes referred to as the generation gap, are wider and deeper than ever before. According to a recent Pew Research Center study, almost 80 percent of adults see a difference between the beliefs and points of view of young people and themselves. Asked to identify where older and younger people differ the most, 47 percent pinpointed the areas of social values and morality.[3]

Consider just some of what today's Christian young people believe:

- 23 percent are not assured of the existence of miracles
- 33 percent either "definitely" or "maybe" believe in reincarnation
- 42 percent are not assured of the existence of evil as an entity
- 48 percent believe that many religions are true[4]

Hopefully your children aren't among those who hold those views, but you can see how it would be easy for kids to adopt unorthodox beliefs when nearly one out of two can't say that Jesus is definitely "the way, the truth and the life." And count on it, your kids are hearing all kinds of unorthodox beliefs.

In the last seven to eight years militant atheists have exploded onto the public scene. For example, Sam Harris began his atheistic assault with the release of *Letter to a Christian Nation* (2006), which was followed by Richard Dawkins's *The God Delusion* (2006), and finally Christopher Hitchens's *God Is Not Great* (2007). All three books quickly experienced explosive sales, spending months—not weeks—on multiple bestseller lists.

The influence of these so-called New Atheists has gone far beyond the publishing world. They have written articles, spoken on college campuses, participated in debates, been interviewed on radio and TV, and posted countless videos on YouTube. They have confused seekers and rocked the faith of many believers. The goal of the New Atheists is simple: to eradicate any rational grounds for religious belief and to persuade theists to walk away from their faith.[5]

Although the New Atheist tide is receding somewhat, still there has never been a time more important than now to equip your kids with why we believe what we believe. But I've had some Christian leaders tell me that today's churched kids aren't interested in the reasons for the Christian faith. They say that all today's kids want is to deal with relationships and what they can experience emotionally.

This simply is not the case. In the recent "National Study of Youth and Religion," thousands of nonreligious teenagers said they were raised to be "religious" but had become "nonreligious." These teenagers were asked, "Why did you fall away from the faith in which you were raised?" They were given no set of answers to pick from; it was an open-ended question. The most common answer—given by 32 percent of the respondents—was *intellectual skepticism.*[6] That is a very high percentage given that this was an open-ended question. Their answers included such statements as "It didn't make sense to me"; "Some stuff is too far-fetched for me to believe in"; "I think scientifically there is no real proof"; "There were too many questions that can't be answered." Our kids want answers they can grapple with in their *minds* as well as in their hearts.

Passing On Your Faith

It is vitally important to ground your kids in what you believe as a Christian and why you believe it. But what are the beliefs you want to pass on to your kids and where did they come from?

I suspect that you want to pass on a faith to your kids that works. You probably want them to embrace a Christianity that is truly Christian, one that changes their lives and one they in turn pass on to their children. This is actually what Christian discipleship is all about, and it is what the early church did so successfully.

The early Christians were so intensely discipled in their beliefs that not only did they experience genuine happiness in their lives, they also successfully passed the baton of the faith from one generation to the next in a movement that expanded like wildfire. Alan Hirsch, founder of Forge Mission Training Network, says that by

AD 100, about 65 years after Jesus was on earth, there were as few as 25,000 Christians. Within 200 years their number exploded to 20 million.[7] That is an increase of 800 times! What did these early Christians pass on that caused such astonishing change and growth to happen?

By the third century there was a focused consensus within the Christian community as to what the truths of the faith were all about. The apostles had set forth certain beliefs that defined how a Christ-follower would live. In order to retain this consensus and prevent a drifting of truth, 300 Church Fathers met in the city of Nicaea in Asia Minor in AD 325 to affirm in writing the essential truths of the Christian faith. The result is what we know as the Nicene Creed. These men produced what is now the most widely used statement of faith ever written. It has been endorsed and accepted by practically every major Christian community in history. In this succinct statement the Nicaean Council captured the truth of who God is and who we are in relationship with him, what he did and our purpose in life, and what his mission is and where we are going. (See the copy of the Nicene Creed that's included at the end of this chapter.)

As you lead your kids into a relationship with God, you can guide them to embrace their Christian beliefs. As they do they will begin to truly understand themselves (who they are, why they are here, and where they are going), how they are to relate to others, and how they are to interact with the natural world God has given them. To give a succinct description of the Christian faith, we could say that *Christianity is a way of knowing and being and living in right relationship with God, ourselves, others, and the world around us.* It is Christ's "way" that we must regain and pass on to our children.

What We Believe and Why We Believe It

When you read over the Nicene Creed you will find 12 beliefs that the apostles "handed down to the saints." All of them are clearly explained in Scripture. And Scripture is where we must begin.

The Bible provides us a clear picture, through many stories, of how God has related to us throughout human history—to the first human family, to the children of Israel in the Old Testament, and to the people who came to know Jesus and his "way" in the New Testament. These stories are God's means of conveying to us who he is. They give us vivid pictures of godly people believing and living out his great truths. These stories and the truths they present define who we are, how God wants to relate to us and us to him, and how we are to relate to one another. All this was committed to sacred writings that are now our reliable Scripture. God himself has preserved these truths for us so we can know him and pass the baton of the faith to our kids.

Unlock the Scripture and it provides a depiction of a specific way of life, a way of knowing what is true, a picture of being what God meant us to be, and a pattern of living based on the revelation of who he is in relationship to us. Or to put it another way, Scripture reveals everything we need to know to see the truth about what the world was meant to be, what it is now, and how it can be restored to his original intention. Scripture shows us that we were originally designed to be in relationship with God, what caused us to lose that relationship, and how it can be reclaimed.

The early church broke all that down into a catechism of sorts, through which Christians taught 12 truths to their children in a relational way. Stated succinctly, Christians believe these 12 truths:

1. A relational God exists.

2. God's Word is an accurate revelation of him.

3. Original sin brought death (separation from God) to the human race.

4. God became human to restore us to a relationship with him.

5. Christ atoned for our sin by dying on the cross.

6. We are justified before God by his grace through faith in Jesus.

7. We are to be transformed into the image of Christ.

8. Jesus rose bodily from the dead.

9. God exists eternally as three Persons in One (the Trinity).

10. God's kingdom forms our view of the world (worldview).

11. The church is Christ's visible representative on earth.

12. Jesus will return to restore all things to God's original design.

It is important to understand that these 12 beliefs or truths aren't something we simply believe with our minds. They are to be lived out in our lives. We don't present what we believe and why we believe it to our kids just so they can think correctly. We want them also to have right relationships and correct living. So we also need to understand why these beliefs are relevant to our lives and why we can trust them to be true. Our kids need to know that what we believe can be supported by evidence.

Sounds like a tall order, doesn't it? And in some respects it is. But when you break these core beliefs down and see how they all connect, you can understand it really is the great story of God redeeming his lost children.

To help you present to your kids what we believe and why we believe it, my son, Sean, and I wrote what I call my defining work. It is entitled *The Unshakable Truth: How You Can Experience the 12 Essentials of a Relevant Faith.** I encourage you to get it, study it, and systematically present to your kids the 12 relevant beliefs of

---

* *The Unshakable Truth* draws on my books *New Evidence That Demands a Verdict, Beyond Belief to Convictions, More Than a Carpenter, Right from Wrong, Why Wait?, How to Be a Hero to Your Kids,* and more. You can check it out at www.josh.org by clicking on "Resources"—and also in the back of this book.

You will also find "why we believe what we believe" books and material for teens and younger children on my website and later in this book. Recently my son and I put together a book providing answers to the most-asked questions about God and the Bible. It can be a valuable tool to help you answer some of the tough questions your kids are going to come up with. Take a look on the website—it's called *77 FAQs About God and the Bible.* It can strengthen your and your kids' faith. You can also find out more about it in the back of this book.

Christianity and why they can so confidently embrace each of them. There is solid evidence that God wants us to discover for each of the core beliefs of Christianity.

Now, examining the evidence for our faith doesn't eliminate the need for faith. No amount of evidence gives us 100 percent certainty. We are still required to exercise our faith, but it should be an intelligent faith that examines the evidence. In fact, that is one of the reasons the apostles recorded the many miraculous signs performed by Jesus: "These [signs] are written so that you may continue to believe that Jesus is the Messiah" (John 20:31).

Jesus also invited people to examine the evidence for believing in him. He said, "Believe that I am in the Father and the Father is in me. Or at least believe because of the work you have seen me do" (John 14:11). When our kids learn the evidences for why they can believe, it gives understanding and strengthens their faith. And when they know how it is relevant to their everyday lives, they can begin to live it out.

The Three Pillars of the Faith

Although there are 12 beliefs within the Nicene Creed, three act as the pillars of the faith. Helping your kids know why they can confidently believe these three core truths will ground them in the faith.

- The first pillar is the reliability of Scripture. If the Bible cannot be trusted as a reliable historical document then we have no assurance that what we believe is even true. Practically everything we believe within Christianity is based upon the Bible.

- The second pillar is the deity of Christ. If Christ was not who he claimed to be then he was not the Holy Lamb of God and could not be our atonement for sin.

- The third pillar is Christ's bodily resurrection. Without his rising from the dead, our own resurrection from the dead is not possible and an eternity without sin and suffering is impossible. The apostle Paul put it this way, "If Christ has not been raised, then your faith is useless, and you are still under condemnation for your sins...[and] we are the most miserable people in the world" (1 Corinthians 15:17,19 NLT).

In the remainder of this chapter I will give you an abbreviated example of what we believe about the Bible and why. Again, I encourage you to take advantage of resources. My team has created three presentations on the pillars that are designed for your family (or a group of families) to share over a meal. The first, which offers evidence for the reliability of Scripture, is called the "Redemption Celebration"; the second, on the deity of Christ, is called the "Revelation Celebration"; and the third, on the evidence for Christ's resurrection, is called the "Restoration Celebration."*

The following is drawn directly from the family Revelation Celebration. This download includes interactive presentations for your kids, such as the "Verbal Relay Process." You may have played the telephone game when you were young. Someone whispers a short sentence in the ear of the person next to him or her and that person whispers what he or she heard to the next person and so on. The last person whispered to repeats the short sentence aloud. Of course the sentence and meaning becomes jumbled and incoherent in transmission.

The little game makes the point that if a message is going to get passed on accurately from one person to another, each word must be clearly and accurately transmitted. This illustrates the importance of the Bible's being carefully and accurately copied by hand from one generation to another. If this wasn't the case, then we have no assurance that what we read today is what was written down thousands of

---

* These free downloadable resources give you everything you need to make a fascinating and clear presentation of why we can believe in the three pillars of the faith. You can find these by going to www.josh.org/RC1; www.josh.org/RC2; and www.josh.org/RC3.

years ago. The Revelation Celebration enables you to provide solid evidence that God's Word is truly reliable.

The download provides a handout that you copy and give to your family. They follow along as you read. The information you go over with your kids demonstrates the care with which God miraculously supervised the transmission of Scripture. It drives home the point that his Word is the most reliable book in all antiquity. He wants us to see him for who he is, and that requires an accurate and undistorted revelation of him—the Holy Bible.

Following is the reading from the Revelation Celebration handout.

God's Word Is Reliable

God spoke to men thousands of years ago and had them write down very important messages he wanted us to know. Because he loved us and wanted a relationship with us, he wanted us to know how we could get to know him. All of us as humans had sinned and were separated from him, so his Word was to become our instructions, or set of love letters from him, on how to come to know him personally.

Do we have an accurate set of love letters? Were the copies made of the original writings done accurately? Let's find out.

The case of the meticulous scribes. Hand-copying of the Old Testament was the responsibility of a group of men who were trained as skilled scribes and gave their lives to writing. For many years before and after the time of Jesus it was their responsibility to copy the Hebrew Scriptures. These particular scribes devoted themselves to making sure that the Holy Scriptures were copied letter for letter, word for word. Their rules for copying Scripture were so strict that when a copy was made it was considered to be an exact duplicate, just as if you had made it from a copy machine. When a copy was finished it was called a manuscript.

A scribe would begin his day of transcribing a manuscript by ceremonially washing his entire body. He would then robe himself in full Jewish dress before sitting down at his desk. As he wrote, if he came to the Hebrew name of God, he could not begin writing the name with a pen newly dipped in ink for fear it would smear the page. Once he began writing the name of God, he could not stop or allow himself to be distracted…even if a king were to enter the room. The scribe was obligated to continue without interruption until he finished penning the holy name of the one true God.

The Masoretic (the Masoretes were a lineage of scribes working in the middle of the first millennium) guidelines for copying manuscripts also required that

- the scroll be written on the skin of a clean animal
- each skin contain a specified number of columns, equal throughout the entire book
- the length of each column extend no less than 48 lines and no more than 60
- the column width consist of exactly 30 letters
- the space of a thread appear between every consonant
- the breadth of nine consonants be inserted between each section
- a space of three lines appear between each book
- the fifth book of Moses (Deuteronomy) conclude exactly with a full line
- nothing—not even the shortest word—be copied from memory, but rather letter by letter
- the scribe count the number of times each letter of the alphabet occurred in each book and compare it to the original
- if a manuscript was found to contain even one mistake, it be discarded [8]

God instilled in the Masoretes such a painstaking reverence for the Hebrew Scriptures in order to ensure the amazingly accurate transmission of the Bible, so you and I would have an accurate revelation of him.

The case of the accurate New Testament. The Hebrew scribes did not copy the manuscripts of the New Testament. So God did a new thing to ensure that the words of Jesus and his followers would be preserved accurately for us: he provided thousands of early manuscripts as sources.

To tell if ancient manuscripts are reliable, scholars 1) measure the time between the original writing and the first manuscript copy; and 2) determine how many manuscript copies are still in existence. The shorter the time between the original writing and the first copy and the more manuscripts there are, the more accurate scholars consider the manuscripts.

For example, virtually everything we know today about Julius Caesar's campaigns in Gaul comes from ten manuscript copies of *The Gallic Wars*, the earliest of which dates to just within 1000 years of the time it was originally written. The most reliably documented writing in secular history is Homer's *Iliad*, with 1757 manuscripts, the earliest of which dates to within 400 years of the original writing.

Let's look at this chart of classical literature. [9]

Author	Book	Date written	Earliest copies	Time gap	Number of copies
Homer	*Iliad*	800 BC	c. 400 BC	c. 400 years	1757
Herodotus	*History*	480–425 BC	c. AD 900	c. 1350 years	8
Thucydides	*History*	460–400 BC	c. AD 900	c. 1300 years	8
Plato		400 BC	c. AD 900	c. 1300 years	7

Author	Book	Date written	Earliest copies	Time gap	Number of copies
Demosthenes		300 BC	c. AD 1100	c. 1400 years	200
Caesar	*Gallic Wars*	100– 44 BC	c. AD 900	c. 1000 years	10
Livy	*History of Rome*	59 BC– AD 17	fourth century (partial); mostly tenth century	c. 400 years c. 1000 years	1 partial 19 copies
Tacitus	*Annals*	AD 100	c. AD 1100	c. 1000 years	20
Pliny Secundus	*Natural History*	AD 61–113	c. AD 850	c. 750 years	7

The New Testament has no equal. Using this accepted standard for evaluating the reliability of ancient writings, the New Testament stands alone. It has no equal. No other book of the ancient world can even compare to the reliability of the New Testament. Take a look at this chart: [10]

Author	Book	Earliest copies	Time gap	Number of copies
John	Gospel of John	c. AD 130	50-plus years	Fragments
Various	The rest of the New Testament books	c. AD 200 (books)	100 years	
		c. AD 250 (most of New Testament)	150 years	
		c. AD 325 (complete New Testament)	225 years	5600- plus Greek manuscripts

Author	Book	Earliest copies	Time gap	Number of copies
		c. AD 366–384 (Latin Vulgate translation)	284 years	
		c. AD 400–500 (other translations)	400 years	19,000-plus translated manuscript
		TOTALS	50–400 years	24,600-plus manuscripts

There are nearly 25,000 manuscripts or fragments of manuscripts, with some dating back to within 50 years of the original writings. And none are more than 400 years newer than the originals. Incredible!

When you hold a Bible in your hand you can be sure it is the most accurate and reliable writing in all of history! God wanted you to be sure that the Bible you read consists of the accurate love letters he had written just for you.

Repeat Them Again and Again

We want to be a valuable resource to you as you ground your kids in why they believe what they believe. I have spent over 50 years trying to help church leaders and dads like you to pass on an intelligent faith to your kids. But this isn't done through one presentation or even a set number of instructional meetings with your kids. It will involve a continual and continuing process.

To effectively teach your kids the precepts of why they believe what they believe will require that you "repeat them again and again to your children. Talk about them when you are at home and when you are on the road, when you are going to bed and when you are getting up" (Deuteronomy 6:7). As you do you will be fulfilling Commitment #9 with the hope that you are raising up "children of God without fault in a crooked and depraved generation. Then [they] will shine among them like stars in the sky" (Philippians 2:15 NIV).

The Nicene Creed

We believe in one God, the Father Almighty, Maker of heaven and earth, and of all things visible and invisible;

And in one Lord Jesus Christ, the only begotten Son of God, begotten of his Father before all worlds, God of God, Light of Light, very God of very God, begotten, not made, being of one substance with the Father; by whom all things were made; who for us men and for our salvation came down from heaven, and was incarnate by the Holy Spirit of the Virgin Mary, and was made man; and was crucified also for us under Pontius Pilate; he suffered and was buried; and the third day he rose again according to the Scriptures, and ascended into heaven, and is seated at the right hand of the Father; and he shall come again, with glory, to judge both the living and the dead; whose kingdom shall have no end.

And we believe in the Holy Ghost, the Lord and giver of life, who proceeds from the Father and the Son; who with the Father and the Son together is worshipped and glorified; who spoke by the prophets. And we believe in the holy catholic and apostolic church; we acknowledge one baptism for the remission of sins; and look for the resurrection of the dead, and the life of the world to come.

12

I Will Do My Best to Foster a Heart of Gratitude

I t's not fair. Why does he get to do it and not me?"
   "I deserved it more than she does."
   "You owe me! Come on, I'm entitled to more than that."

It seems a good number of people in our society possess a sense of entitlement—a feeling they are owed things by right rather than having to work for them. You can hear and see expressions of entitlement almost every day in society, often reflected by an ungrateful spirit.

The quotes above reflect an ungrateful attitude. You may even detect such an attitude coming from your own kids. Sure, it's natural for them to expect certain things and complain when they don't get them. Yet if a complaining, ungrateful attitude becomes part of their mindset and disposition, it can have a far-reaching negative effect. A person with an ungrateful heart has a high probability of experiencing high levels of stress, discouragement, and depression, as well as a greater difficulty in forming healthy relationships. Overall the person will experience less satisfaction with his or her life. And there are studies to document that.

I started off this book by asking you what you want for your kids. I suggested it is probably what Jesus wants for all of us. He wants his joy to be in us and our joy to be complete (see John 15:11). We want to see our kids enjoy life too, don't we? We want them to be protected from harm and become individuals with a sense of meaning, purpose, and fulfillment in life. Beyond committing their lives to Christ, I contend that one of the best ways to help them achieve that is to foster within them a heart of gratitude.

Doing this for your kids will pay huge dividends in very specific areas of their lives. Recently, scientists have conducted research aimed at understanding the positive effects of being grateful. For instance, in 2012 the University of California, Berkeley, began collaborating with the University of California, Davis, in a $5.6 million, three-year project called "Expanding the Science and Practice of Gratitude."[1] The idea is to find ways to promote practices of gratitude in medical, educational, and organizational settings to reap the benefits of being grateful.

Dr. Robert Emmons, a leading scientific expert on gratitude, contends that hundreds of studies have documented its social, physical, and psychological benefits. He points out that practicing gratitude

- increases happiness and life satisfaction
- reduces anxiety and depression
- strengthens the immune system, lowers blood pressure, reduces symptoms of illness, and makes us less bothered by aches and pains
- helps us sleep better
- makes us more resilient, helping us recover more effectively from traumatic events
- strengthens relationships, making us feel closer and more connected to friends, family, and spouses[2]

In other words, when we become grateful individuals we develop better ways of coping with difficulties and handling stress in life. For example, grateful people tend to handle failure and negative circumstances with less stress and embrace success with more grace. Dr. Melanie Greenberg, clinical and health psychologist, says that practicing gratitude "opens the heart and activates positive emotion centers in the brain. Regular practice of gratitude can change the way our brain neurons fire into more positive automatic patterns."[3]

Is it any wonder God's Word tells us to "be thankful in all circumstances, for this is God's will for you who belong to Christ Jesus" (1 Thessalonians 5:18)? God wants us to live a life of joy. Being grateful is foundational to experiencing true joy. "Give thanks to the LORD, for he is good!" wrote the psalmist. "His faithful love endures forever" (Psalm 136:1).

The Scriptures admonish us over a thousand times in many different ways to be thankful, praise God, rejoice, and have a grateful heart. In fact God's command to worship him is an instruction to acknowledge him for who he is and what he has provided and in response give him praise and honor and love. "Give thanks for everything to God the Father in the name of our Lord Jesus Christ" (Ephesians 5:20). Yet gratefulness doesn't happen automatically with us. When things aren't going very well it's not easy to be grateful. Gratefulness is a quality that has to be cultivated.

Gratitude Must Be Cultivated

In my early Christian life the idea of gratefulness wasn't really on my radar. I knew I was to praise God and be thankful, but I didn't see it as being foundational to my Christian walk. In other words, I didn't see a connection between a heart of gratitude and living a life of joy even though Jesus said he was there to make my joy complete. But my perspective on practicing gratitude changed after a life-altering experience.

After I finished seminary, I joined Campus Crusade for Christ, hoping to become a traveling youth speaker. Back then I was bold, aggressive, and a little cocky. My heart was in the right place, but I didn't have a lot of patience. I wanted to be cut loose to travel and speak. Yet the leaders over me felt I needed more maturity.

In my zeal I inadvertently offended some of these leaders. In fact my aggressiveness gave them problems. So they saw to it that I got an unusual assignment. Rather than assigning me to a speaking tour in the U.S. they sent me to Argentina to work on a university campus.

This turn of events was more than disappointing to me. I was nearly devastated. It represented more than a delay of my hopes and plans; it felt like a setback. At the time, I didn't at all feel grateful to anyone and had little to be thankful for. Of course this negative thinking failed to take into consideration that God was about to cause things to work together for my good and his glory.

I did accept the assignment. And the more I prayed about it the more I began to realize I needed to be faithful to the task I was given and leave my future in God's hands. I had read the wise words of Solomon, who said that God "is a shield to those who walk with integrity. He guards the paths of the just and protects those who are faithful to him" (Proverbs 2:7-8). I wanted to be a faithful servant.

When I arrived in Argentina in 1967, the South American universities were hotbeds of Communist activity. Brash and zealous, as always, I jumped in with both feet and went head-to-head in open debate with the revolutionaries on those campuses. I traveled beyond Argentina to campuses in Bolivia and Chile. During the two-year period of attempting to establish a campus ministry in South America, my life was repeatedly threatened. I was robbed, framed for a crime, and imprisoned. At times I wondered if I would ever make it home alive.

News of what God was accomplishing in South America got back to Dr. Bill Bright, president of Campus Crusade at the time. The leadership I had offended had moved on. The new leadership asked if I would return to the United States to launch a speaking tour to university students. My hopes and dreams were about to come true. King David was right: "Take delight in the LORD, and he will give you your heart's desires" (Psalm 37:4).

When I returned to the United States, American universities were just beginning to experience the kind of unrest and upheaval I had seen and studied for two years on South American campuses. My experience in Argentina had equipped me to understand what the revolutionaries were offering as a cultural solution to American youth and prepared me to effectively counter that with a spiritual solution. I watched in amazement as it turned out that my two years in "exile" were God's "boot camp" to bring him honor for the next 20 years of my campus ministry. It was a life lesson to be grateful in whatever circumstances I find myself and keep my trust in God's plan for my life.

Seven Ways to Foster Gratitude in Your Kids

Here are seven practical ways to help teach your kids to have a grateful heart.

1. Teach your kids to be faithful and trust in God's plan. I have used my South American "exile" story many times to help my kids realize that God does have a plan for their lives. I have told them the key is to trust in his plan and be faithful regardless of the circumstances. I had learned that my circumstances weren't to determine whether I was grateful or not. I was to be grateful by faith in God's plan. He would receive honor regardless of what happened to me. A heart of gratitude was to be a constant in my life regardless of my circumstances.

Lead your kids to trust in a God who has control of our lives. Have them memorize Romans 8, which tell us that "we know that God causes everything to work together for the good of those who love God and are called according to his purpose for them" (Romans 8:28). That doesn't mean everything that happens will be good, but if we are faithful, he will be honored even out of the most difficult situation. Like Joseph who was sold into slavery, we can say, "As far as I am concerned, God turned into good what [others] meant for evil" (Genesis 50:20 NLT).

2. Teach your kids to recognize their total lostness. When you teach your kids why they believe the 12 core beliefs of Christianity, you will encounter the one on original sin. Use that belief as a foundation to being grateful.

When you explain that we are all sinners and separated from God, explain that our lostness eliminates any sense of entitlement. In his perfect justice we have no right to enjoy a relationship with him. There is nothing good in us to even justify his mercy. "No one is good—not even one..." the Scripture states. "All have turned away from God; all have gone wrong. No one does good, not even one" (Romans 3:10,12 NLT).

Recognizing our total lostness and condition as sinners helps us realize we can do nothing in ourselves to merit God's grace. Realizing we can't do a thing to merit mercy from him produces an overwhelming sense of gratefulness when he offers his mercy.

3. Teach your kids to marvel at God's amazing grace. Explain this to your kids:

God took on human form in the person of Jesus and died a horrible death because of your sin. He did that for you when you were an unrepentant sinner. You rejected him, yet he still accepted you. It's like Jesus is saying, "You may have turned away from me, but I'm not turning away from you. You are so important to me that I will go to extraordinary lengths to have a personal relationship with you. I'll enter your world and become human like you to save you from death and eternal aloneness without me."

Repeat that wonderful grace-filled story of Jesus dying so unjustly to your kids over and over again. Help them to marvel at God's amazing grace. When we truly recognize the extent of our lostness and realize the extent of his mercy it fosters a heart of gratitude.

4. Teach your kids to allow work to fuel gratefulness. Jesus said, "Those who work deserve their pay" (Luke 10:7). Paul said, "Never be lazy, but work hard and serve the Lord enthusiastically" (Romans 12:11). Dottie and I made it a practice to give our kids an allowance based on chores they were assigned to do. When your kids are taught to be part of the team to keep the house clean, mow the lawn, and other household chores they are more grateful for the allowance they receive. Help your kids appreciate the rewards of their labor. There are times for gifts, but good hard work is meant to fuel a grateful heart.

5. Teach your kids to keep expectations low. There are numerous benefits in lowering people's expectations and then exceeding them. One is that people are gratefully surprised. The same is true when it comes to giving gifts to your kids or raising expectations about a vacation. Teach your kids to keep their expectations low in receiving gifts from you. That will give you a greater chance of exceeding your kids' expectations, and then they can enjoy the thrill of being gratefully surprised.

Dottie and I always tried to keep our kids' expectations low as to what they might get on Christmas or birthdays or what we could do on vacation. It's a good policy. When you succeed at doing that, it helps cultivate a grateful heart in the life of your kids.

6. Teach your kids to create a daily thankful list. Make it a practice to ask your kids what they're thankful for, each day if you can. Being thankful as a family isn't just for Thanksgiving Day, it's for every day. "This is the day the LORD has made," the Scripture says. "We will rejoice and be glad in it" (Psalm 118:24). Get your kids to exercise their grateful hearts daily by verbally expressing what they are grateful for even in the little things of life. As you do you will be fostering within them a heart of gratitude.

7. Teach your kids to be a model of gratitude. Let your kids sense your heart of gratitude and hear you express thanks every day. Dad, set the tone of a grateful spirit by expressing a constant sense of gratitude for everything: the food your family eats, the roof over your head, the car you drive, the wife you have, the sun that shines, the flowers that grow, and so on. The more they see you praise God for all his protection and provision and sense your thankful heart, the more likely they too will become a living model of gratefulness.

"I Will Do My Best"

Make the 10 Commitments presented in this book part of your life with your kids. As you do, you will be imparting a part of yourself to them. Remember these truths are to be spoken in love out of a heart of love. It isn't just about getting some good ideas in their heads—rather it's about enabling them to wrap their hearts around a way of life.

My kids are all grown and raising families of their own. When I look back on their childhood years I can't say I did everything right. No one can. But what I say—and you can say too—is that we did our best with what we knew at the time.

As I interact with my grandchildren I notice I have a lot more patience and wisdom than I had when my kids were at home. About the time I got my act together as a dad, the kids were grown and out of the house. But that is the way it is supposed to be. Being a dad will always be an on-the-job training program. Take advantage of all the resources you can get your hands on and do the best you can. God will reward you for it.

Relational Needs
Assessment Inventory

Instructions

For each of the 50 statements below, enter the number that best represents your response to that statement. Then you may interpret your responses by completing the section "Identifying Your Top Needs." Ask your wife to take this inventory as well. If you have teenagers they can probably relate to most of the assessment test. Ask them to take it as well. You will probably need to score younger children by assessing how they would respond to each statement.

Strongly Disagree	Disagree	Neutral	Agree	Strongly Agree
-2	-1	0	+1	+2

___1. It is important that people accept me for who I am, even if I'm a little "different."

___2. It is very important to me that my financial world be in order.

___3. I sometimes grow weary of doing my usual best.

___4. It is important to me that others seek my opinion.

____5. It is important that I receive frequent physical hugs, warm embraces, and so on.

____6. I feel good when someone enters into my world and wants to know what I'm all about.

____7. It is important for me to know where I stand with those who are in authority over me.

____8. It is meaningful to me when someone notices that I need help and offers to get involved.

____9. I often feel overwhelmed. When this happens, I need someone to come alongside me and lighten my load.

____10. I feel blessed when someone notices and shows concern for how I'm doing emotionally.

____11. I like to know if what I do is of value to others.

____12. Generally speaking, I don't like a lot of solitude.

____13. It means a lot to me when loved ones initiate an "I love you."

____14. I resist being seen only as a part of a large group. Being recognized as an individual is important to me.

____15. I feel blessed when someone calls just to hear me out and encourages me.

____16. It is important to me that people acknowledge not only what I do but who I am.

____17. I feel best when my world is orderly and somewhat predictable.

___18. I am pleased when people acknowledge my work on a project and express gratitude.

___19. I especially enjoy completing a task when I am surrounded by others who like being with me.

___20. I feel good when others notice my strengths and gifts.

___21. I sometimes feel overwhelmed and discouraged.

___22. I want to be treated with kindness and equality by all, regardless of my race, gender, looks, and status.

___23. Physical affection in marriage is very important to me.

___24. I love it when someone wants to spend time with me alone.

___25. I feel blessed when someone notices what I do and says, "Good job!"

___26. It is meaningful to me to be held and cared for after a hard day.

___27. Even when I am confident about my talents, gifts, and so on, I welcome input and help from others.

___28. When I feel stressed out or down, sympathy and encouragement from other people are very meaningful to me.

___29. I feel good when someone expresses satisfaction with the way I am.

___30. I enjoy being in a group of people when they are talking positively about me.

___31. I would describe myself as a touchy-feely person.

____**32.** It is important that my input is considered in a decision that will affect my life or schedule.

____**33.** I feel blessed when someone shows interest in the projects I am working on.

____**34.** I like trophies, plaques, and special gifts which commemorate something significant I have done.

____**35.** I sometimes worry about the future.

____**36.** When in a new environment, I immediately search for a group of people to connect with.

____**37.** The thought of moving, starting a new job or class, or making other changes fills me with anxiety.

____**38.** It bothers me when people are prejudiced against others because they dress or act differently.

____**39.** I need to be surrounded by friends and loved ones who will be there through thick and thin.

____**40.** I feel blessed when someone thanks me for something I have done.

____**41.** It is very meaningful to me to know that someone is praying for me.

____**42.** I am bothered by people who try to control others.

____**43.** I feel blessed when I receive undeserved and spontaneous expressions of love.

____**44.** I am pleased when someone looks me in the eyes and really listens when I talk.

___**45.** I feel blessed when people commend me for any godly characteristic I exhibit.

___**46.** It is important to me to have a soul mate stand with me when I am hurting or in trouble.

___**47.** I don't enjoy working alone. I would rather have someone working with me.

___**48.** It is important to me to feel like I am a part of the group.

___**49.** I respond positively when someone seeks to understand my emotions and shows me loving concern.

___**50.** When working on a project, I would much rather work with a team of people than by myself.

Identifying Your Top Needs

INSTRUCTIONS:

Using the numbers (-2, -1, 0, +1, +2) that you placed in the blank in front of each item in the **Relational Needs Assessment Inventory**, add up the numbers to discover what your total is for each of the ten relational needs.

ACCEPTANCE

1. Add up your response (-2, -1, 0, +1, +2) to statements:

1 _____
19 _____
36 _____
38 _____
48 _____
Total _____

These responses relate to the need for *acceptance.*

SECURITY

2. Add up your responses to statements:

2 _____
17 _____
35 _____
37 _____
39 _____
Total _____

These responses relate to the need for *security.*

APPRECIATION

3. Add up your responses to statements:

16 _____
18 _____
20 _____
34 _____
40 _____
Total _____

These responses relate to the need for *appreciation.*

ENCOURAGEMENT

4. Add up your responses to statements:

3 _____
15 _____
21 _____
33 _____
41 _____
Total _____

These responses relate to the need for *encouragement.*

Respect

5. Add up your responses
   to statements:

   4 _____
   14 _____
   22 _____
   32 _____
   42 _____
   Total _____

   These responses relate to the
   need for *respect.*

Affection

6. Add up your responses
   to statements:

   5 _____
   13 _____
   23 _____
   31 _____
   43 _____
   Total _____

   These responses relate to the
   need for *affection.*

Attention

7. Add up your responses
   to statements:

   6 _____
   12 _____
   24 _____
   30 _____
   44 _____
   Total _____

   These responses relate to the
   need for *attention.*

Approval

8. Add up your responses
   to statements:

   7 _____
   11 _____
   25 _____
   29 _____
   45 _____
   Total _____

   These responses relate to the
   need for *approval.*

COMFORT

9. Add up your responses
to statements:

10	_____
26	_____
28	_____
46	_____
49	_____
Total	_____

These responses relate to the
need for *comfort.*

SUPPORT

10. Add up your responses
to statements:

8	_____
9	_____
27	_____
47	_____
50	_____
Total	_____

These responses relate to the
need for *support.*

Notes

Chapter One: What's a Dad to Do?

1. "Teens Look to Parents More Than Friends," *Science Daily*, June 15, 2011, http://sciencedaily.com/releases/2011/06/110615120355.htm.

2. "Teens Look to Parents."

3. Jeffrey Rosenberg and W. Bradford Wilcox, "The Importance of Fathers in the Healthy Development of Children," publication of U.S. Department of Health and Human Services, 2006, http://childwelfare.gov/pubs/usermanuals /father-hood/fatherhood.pdf.

4. "Talking to Your Teen About Sexuality," publication of Hillsborough County University of Florida Extension, http://hillsboroughfcs.ifas.ufl.edu/ FamilyPubsA-Z/sexuality.pdf.

Chapter Two: Commitment #1: I Will Do My Best to Always Speak the Truth in Love

1. Josh and Dottie McDowell, *Straight Talk with Your Kids About Sex* (Eugene, OR: Harvest House Publishers, 2012), 45-46.

2. The Commission on Children at Risk, *Hardwired to Connect: The Scientific Case for Authoritative Communications* (New York: Broadway Publications, 2003).

Chapter Three: Commitment #2: I Will Do My Best to Be Responsible *to* My Kids Rather Than *for* Them: First Part

1. In the first edition, 1996.

2. Drawn from Josh McDowell and Sean McDowell, *Experience Your Bible* (Eugene, OR: Harvest House Publishers, 2012), 45-46.

Chapter Six: Commitment #4: I Will Do My Best to Explain Who God Is and What He Is Like

1. Howard Culbertson, "When Americans Become Christian," research publication of Southern Nazarene University, August 26, 2009, http://home .snu.edu/~hculbert/ages.htm.

Chapter Seven: Commitment #5: I Will Do My Best to Instill a Love of Self That Is Unselfish

1. Walter Bruce, *A Greek-English Lexicon of the New Testament* (Chicago: University of Chicago Press, 1957), 874.

2. Charles Caldwell Ryrie, ed., *Ryrie Study Bible* (Chicago: Moody Press, 1976), 25.

Chapter Ten: Commitment #8: I Will Do My Best to Teach How to Honor God's Design for Sex

1. Marcela Raffaelli, Karen Bogenschneider, and Mary Fran Flood, "Parent-Teen Communication about Sexual Topics," *Journal of Family Issues*, vol. 19, 315-333.

2. Adapted from chapter 11 of Josh and Dottie McDowell, *Straight Talk with Your Kids about Sex* (Eugene, OR: Harvest House Publishers, 2012), 89-90.

3. McDowell, adapted from chapter 2, 26-31.

4. McDowell, adapted from chapter 3, 35-43.

Chapter Eleven: Commitment #9: I Will Do My Best to Present Why We Believe What We Believe

1. Josh McDowell and David H. Bellis, *Last Christian Generation* (Holiday, FL: Green Key Books, 2006), 11-13.

2. David Kinnaman and Gabe Lyons, *unChristian* (Grand Rapids, MI: Baker Books, 2007), 74.

3. Pew Research Center Study, Hope Yen, as cited in "Generation Gap Is Widest Since 1960s," *Akron* (Ohio) *Beacon Journal*, 29 June 2009.

4. Christian Smith, *Soul Searching: The Religious and Spiritual Lives of American Teenagers* (New York: Oxford University Press, 2005), 41-45, 74.

5. Josh McDowell and Sean McDowell, *More Than a Carpenter* (Wheaton, IL: Tyndale House Publishers, 2009), 46.

6. Smith, 89.

7. Alan Hirsch, *The Forgotten Ways* (Grand Rapids, MI: Brazos Press, 2006), 18.

8. Josh McDowell, *The New Evidence That Demands a Verdict* (Nashville, TN: Nelson, 1999), 74.

9. McDowell, *New Evidence*, 38.

10. McDowell, *New Evidence*, 34-39.

Chapter Twelve: Commitment #10: I Will Do My Best to Foster a Heart of Gratitude

1. Steven E.F. Brown, "Thanksgiving: The Power of Gratitude," *San Francisco Business Times*, November 13, 2012.

2. Robert Emmons, "Why Gratitude Is Good," as adapted in "Why Practice Gratitude?" *Greater Good: The Science of a Meaningful Life*, e-newsletter of Greater Good Science Center, Univ. of California, Berkeley, http://greatergood .berkeley.edu/topic/gratitude/definition#how_to_cultivate.

3. As quoted in Melanie Greenberg, "The Mindful Self-Express," *Psychology Today*, November 23, 2011.

About the Author
and the Josh McDowell Ministry

As a young man, **Josh McDowell** was a skeptic of Christianity. However, while at Kellogg College in Michigan, he was challenged by a group of Christian students to intellectually examine the claims of Jesus Christ. Josh accepted the challenge and came face-to-face with the reality that Jesus was in fact the Son of God, who loved him enough to die for him. Josh committed his life to Christ, and for 50 years he has shared with the world both his testimony and the evidence that God is real and relevant to our everyday lives.

Josh received a bachelor's degree from Wheaton College and a master's degree in theology from Talbot Theological Seminary in California. He has been on staff with Cru (formerly Campus Crusade for Christ) for almost 50 years. Josh and his wife, Dottie, have been married for more than 40 years and have four grown children and five grandchildren. They live in Southern California.

Other Resources from
Josh McDowell and Sean McDowell

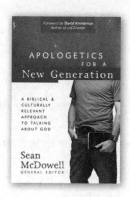

Apologetics for a New Generation
A Biblical and Culturally Relevant Approach to Talking About God
Sean McDowell, general editor

This generation's faith is constantly under attack from the secular media, skeptical teachers, and unbelieving peers. You may wonder, *How can I help?*

Working with young adults every day, Sean McDowell understands their situation and shares your concern. His first-rate team of contributors shows how you can help members of the new generation plant their feet firmly on the truth. Find out how you can walk them through the process of...

- formulating a biblical worldview and applying scriptural principles to everyday issues

- articulating their questions and addressing their doubts in a safe environment

- becoming confident in their faith and effective in their witness

The truth never gets old, but people need to hear it in fresh, new ways. Find out how you can effectively share the answers to life's big questions with a new generation.

The Unshakable Truth®

How You Can Experience the 12 Essentials of a Relevant Faith

Josh McDowell and Sean McDowell

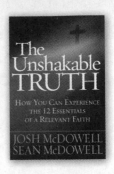

This comprehensive yet easy-to-understand handbook unpacks 12 biblical truths that define the core of Christian belief and Christianity's reason for existence, helping you understand why your faith is meaningful and credible. Discover

- the foundational truths about God, his Word, sin, Christ, the Trinity, the church, and six more that form the bedrock of Christian faith
- how you can live out these truths in relationship with God and others
- ways to pass each truth on to your family and the world around you

Biblically grounded, spiritually challenging, and full of practical examples and real-life stories, *The Unshakable Truth®* is a resource applicable to every aspect of everyday life. *Study guide available.*

77 FAQs About God and the Bible

Your Toughest Questions Answered

Josh McDowell and Sean McDowell

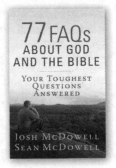

Most of us have honest questions about God and the Bible, but it's sometimes hard to know how to ask them—and who to ask. Through extensive research and insight Josh and Sean McDowell provide answers to issues such as...

- What kinds of proofs are there that God exists?
- Isn't the Bible full of errors and contradictions?

And they tackle tough questions raised by today's skeptics, including...

- If God is so loving, why can't he be more tolerant of sin?
- Isn't it arrogant to claim Christianity is the only true religion?

Concise and accessible, *77 FAQs* gives you solid answers to help you better know why you believe and grow deeper in your faith.

For You and Your Kids Together

The Amazing Bible Adventure for Kids
Finding the Awesome Truth in God's Word
Josh McDowell and Kevin Johnson

Josh McDowell, author of *The Unshakable Truth®* and many others, joins pastor and bestselling author Kevin Johnson to map out a quest for children ages 7 to 11—a quest that will lead them to the discovery that God is truth, and that real happiness comes from knowing him as he is revealed in his Word.

With fun facts, questions, and laugh-out-loud stories, McDowell and Johnson simplify the tough concepts and bring boys and girls to the most amazing treasure of all!

The Awesome Book of Bible Answers for Kids

Josh McDowell and Kevin Johnson

These concise, welcoming answers include key Bible verses and explorations of topics that matter most to kids ages 8 to 12: God's love; right and wrong; Jesus, the Holy Spirit, and God's Word; different beliefs and religions; church, prayer, and sharing faith. Josh and Kevin look at questions like...

- How do I know God wants to be my friend?
- Are parts of the Bible make-believe, or is everything true?
- Was Jesus a wimp?
- Why do some Christians not act like Christians?
- Can God make bad things turn out okay?

The next time a child in your life asks a good question, this practical and engaging volume will give you helpful tips and conversation ideas so you can connect with them and offer straight talk about faith in Jesus. *Includes an easy-to-use learning and conversation guide.*